BEYOND
THE SLOGAN

BEYOND THE SLOGAN

HOW A VIDEO A DAY TAUGHT ME
THE WINNING WAY

KEITH GREIVELDINGER

Beyond the Slogan:
How a Video a Day Taught Me the Winning Way

Copyright © 2021 Keith Greiveldinger
www.thewinitminute.com

BMD Publishing
All Rights Reserved

ISBN # 978-1-7372175-0-3

BMDPublishing@MarketDominationLLC.com
www.MarketDominationLLC.com
Win it Minute Media LLC
www.winitminute.com

BMD Publishing CEO: Seth Greene
Editorial Management: Bruce Corris
Technical Editor & Layout: Kristin Watt

Printed in the United States of America.

ACKNOWLEDGMENTS

To succeed in anything in life it takes the help of others. I have been incredibly fortunate to be surrounded my entire life by inspirational people and continue to thank God for every single person that I have had the opportunity to learn from.

First and foremost, my wife, Elisabeth, who is has been my Rock and given me the greatest gifts of all...love and my children. She pushes me every day to be the best version of myself so that I can be of service in love to my family. I cannot thank my incredible wife enough.

Also, my parents Richard and Phyllis, who have been there for me since the beginning and have never once wavered in their love for me. This love has allowed me to have the confidence to go out into an unstable and crazy world knowing that I am loved and that is the greatest fuel one could ever have.

My children Adrian, Grayson, and Addison. When my son Adrian was born, he had to have open heart surgery which changed my entire perspective on life, and out of this difficult time the Win It Minute mindset was born. I was inspired to live every day with purpose for my children, and if they are the only people to ever read this book and learn from it, then it was worth it because they are the reason I wrote this book.

I love my children with all my heart and would do anything for them, and I hope some day they know just how much Dad truly loves them.

To quote the great Lou Gehrig, "Today, I feel like the luckiest man on the face of the Earth." This is because as I reflect upon of my life, I know that I have been incredibly fortunate to have been surrounded by great friends that made me who I am today. Friends that I have know since kindergarten like Goody, Will, Ryan, Blake and so many more, to friends today that continue to inspire me, including Jack Alan Levine and Jeff Loeffert, I cannot name enough that helped inspire me along the way.

I also want to thank my good friend Brian K. Wright without him this book would never have come to fruition. Brian inspires me every day, and his hard work and wisdom to guide me down this path lead the way to a Winning day.

Lastly, I want to thank God the Heavenly Father as without him nothing would be possible. Every day is a Gift from God that we get to treasure.

Thanks to all for Winning The Day!

TABLE OF CONTENTS

INTRODUCTION

Why Am I Writing This Book?

If you look around at what's going on around us, it can be very easy to feel negative and hopeless at times.

The media always seem to point toward the worst of everything. And why not? They give us what they believe sells and generates the most attention.

However, there is just as much room for positive vibes in the world, and it is needed much more than the negativity that is so easily found.

My main objective in life is to follow my passion and inspire as many others as possible to do the same. I find that whenever we do something that fills us with enthusiasm, we're fulfilling our own legacies.

When I started doing my *Win It Minute* videos in 2016, I did it born out of a realization for the need to inspire people and put out a great message others need to hear. I went through a dark and challenging time and I needed to hear something like this and after fighting through I realized others needed this just like me. Doing this ended up inspiring me even more.

I found that when I do something that I'm passionate about in life—very much like the people I look up to—I get ignited, and it has allowed me to ignite others around me.

I want to spread positivity and impact the world because I've learned so much about the human mind and the power of the mindset that it revolutionized my life and it can yours as well.

No doubt I'm living more or less an average life by many people's standards. But once I started diving into the power of the mindset, everything changed. I want everyone to know that there's a blueprint to success in life, and it all has to do with your mind. You can train your mind to see the world in a different way, and I want to teach others how they can train their mind how to think.

The way I've utilized all these ideas that I've learned is not rocket science. It's quite simple actually, and I want to teach other people how they can implement that in their daily lives.

If you find even one golden nugget that can change your life, then this will be time well invested.

Are you ready?

Let's get started!

CHAPTER
ONE

HOW IT ALL BEGAN

I grew up in a very small, humble town in Wisconsin. My parents didn't give me more than anyone else growing up, yet they gave me everything. Although we didn't have a great amount of money growing up, we made the best of it. My parents always believed in me and provided unconditional love, and that always kept me going.

The most critical thing that I found in life is to keep going and keep moving forward. Their belief in me allowed me to play any sport. Having them in my corner encouraged me to never quit, no matter what happened.

Having someone advocate for you at every turn is critically important.

When I was in school, I wasn't the greatest student, but my mom always believed in me. I just kept moving forward, did all of my homework, made my way through school, and eventually got to college.

I had a lot of different jobs, and I knew that everything I was doing at any given time would eventually lead me to something greater down the line.

At 16 years old, I was working in a stockroom as a supervisor in a liquor store, and I was a liquor salesman's best friend because I wanted to learn as much about liquor as possible. People who walked in the store would ask, "What goes great with a Chardonnay or Cabernet?" and I could answer that question even though I never tasted wine just by simply learning the right answer.

Then when I was in college, I looked for work opportunities in sports because I loved them so much. Honestly, I fell into a PR internship because I was dumb enough to apply for it, even though I wasn't even that interested in it. I was more focused on business as an area of study.

That being said, I got a great opportunity as an intern with the Milwaukee Bucks of the NBA. And that really sparked my interest. I had to collect quotes from players, and ironically, now my favorite thing to do in life is collect quotes. I read them almost every single day and look for ways to apply them to my life. One of the best ways to grow in life is to stand on the shoulders of giants and learn what they did, how they did it, and study the results they achieved. Studying quotes is a great way to get insight into the person who said them. I feel fortunate to have gotten my start at a place where collecting quotes was my job.

That led me to another job for the Great American Shoe Company. The Allen Edmonds factory in my hometown happened to be one of the largest American men's shoe companies. I thought working for them would be a great experience, and I didn't think twice about it. When you decide to take advantage of opportunities, you never know where the road could lead. I just put my head down, worked hard, and moved forward.

I ended up in Dallas, Texas taking a new job, and then that led me to Orlando, Florida, where I currently live. Having a strong passion for sales and sales management led me to read countless books on motivation and psychology. That led me to get into an MBA program from the University of Central Florida when I moved here.

Once you take action on your goals, it's amazing how one thing leads to another. For me, it was all sequenced perfectly, and while I was going through each different moment of my career and my life, I didn't realize how it was setting me up for the next opportunity.

It really started with not having a fear of failure because I always knew that one person in my life believed in me. My mom or my dad always believed in me, and I was lucky because not everyone gets to experience that. I had the courage to do things that seemed unconventional to the standard person and I just kept moving forward. All you need is that one person, and it can even be yourself.

Even though my professional life seemed to be going well, there were challenges at home that my wife and I had to battle through together as a team.

It's amazing to discover that in those moments of adversity, you find out how powerful you really are, and that courage and power come from inspirational sources.

One situation in particular was when my wife and I were trying to start a family. We had trouble conceiving, so we eventually decided to try IVF treatments. I knew in my heart that these treatments would work, although my wife had doubts about it. However, my belief was very strong, and she couldn't believe how calm I was.

During this time, I was traveling on business quite often, and we went through a lot of testing to see what the issues might be. We got the treatment and the doctors injected eggs. To our great joy, we finally had a pregnancy. We were going to have a baby to begin our family

I was on a business trip soon after we heard this news, and on one particular occasion, I was reading a book in my hotel room by Nick Vujicic. He's a faith-based motivational speaker who has no arms and no legs. When I got to the third page—and I'll never forget this—my wife called me and told me that the test came negative now and we lost the baby.

I was so mad at life and the unfair circumstances I felt that we had been dealt, and I actually took the Nick Vujicic book, spit at it, then ripped a couple of pages and threw them in the garbage. At that point, I had decided that all of this mindset, motivational, inspirational stuff was nonsense and didn't work.

In frustration, I threw the entire book in the garbage as well.

I decided that I was done with trying to learn these things. But after five minutes of reflection, I realized, "Oh my God, this guy has overcome having been born with no limbs and I was feeling sorry for myself sitting in this nice hotel room and traveling on business because we didn't get our first child right away".

It was a complete mindset shift. I picked up the book and I still have it to this day, sitting on my bookshelf to remind me of that. Every once in a while, I'll pick up the book and flip it open and look at it. There's still a pattern where I spit at the book, ripped it out, and threw it down. I had a choice to make at that moment as to whether or not I would give in to the anger and the frustration of the unfair world that I was perceiving at the moment or move forward.

I also realized that maybe it was a test to keep moving forward and to keep reading that book. So, I decided to keep reading, and the more I absorbed it, the more it restored my faith. I was inspired to read more. As I learned more about his story and all the obstacles he overcame, it seemed like my troubles and my obstacles were so minuscule in comparison. As a result, I felt guilty about how I previously felt.

That epiphany got me fired up, and that's where the big spark to read motivational books started.

But I know I kept the book for that reason. I spent five minutes being angry, and then I calmed down and shifted back to a better state of mind.

I knew I couldn't remain angry because my wife was also angry. She was upset, so I knew I had to be stronger and overcome this for the both of us. I knew that if I was at home, my reaction may have taken a different path. I may have wallowed in anger with her, or I may have left for a while.

But the realization that I needed to pursue the right mindset and be an example to those around me inspired me to take the next step in my growth.

That step was to impact the world.

The vehicle to doing that began with making daily videos.

CHAPTER TWO

THE IMPACT OF DOING VIDEOS

I started doing videos because I wanted to encourage and inspire others to be the best version of themselves, and when you do anything on a regular basis it becomes a habit. I've found that habits are the most powerful thing you can use to change your circumstances.

Doing these videos forced me to read more inspirational books. If I didn't have that driving force behind wanting to teach others, I wouldn't have kept going. Doing these videos forced me to learn something brand new—not only motivational and inspirational material, but also how to go on camera and communicate effectively in that medium, and how to talk to people and communicate.

It's amazing to look back at the first *Win It Minute* that I ever did. It was on my laptop computer. I was just sitting there talking, and as I look back at that moment, I realize I was so much calmer than I am now.

It's helped me grow into the person that I am now. Life is a reflection—whatever you're sending out into the world comes back to you. As I started doing these positive and inspirational videos that inspired me, I began to notice other people around me were looking at me differently as this "motivational, inspirational" guy.

At that point, I felt like they created this image of me in their minds which may or may not have been who I really was. However, it was so powerful to see them look at me differently, so I wanted to live up to that image and perception so much more. As a result, I worked harder at being a more positive inspirational person. Once you create an image, whether it's true or not, you want to live up to that character because that's how others see you and it becomes a self-fulfilling prophecy in a way.

That realization made me work harder. If I was in a social setting and I was frustrated or angry, I had to remember that I'm the *Win It Minute* guy. When you put yourself out in the public eye, people notice what you do and whether or not your words and actions are consistent. That means that I make a conscious effort to live up to the *Win It Minute* image of being inspirational and positive in all settings. It really helped me redefine who I am, and that's how I found out what I was better at than anything else in my life. It gave me more confidence, too.

People started telling me how much they love that I'm such a positive guy, so when I realized how much people love positivity, I just started ramping that up. The more I did it, the more people liked it, and the more I liked it, the more I liked who I was becoming. It all fed upon itself.

When we create something and people perceive us in a particular way, it gives us something to live up to—and it's all based on how others interpret our actions.

CHAPTER THREE

IF WE CAN CONTROL OUR INTERPRETATIONS, WE CAN CONTROL OUR WORLD

In life, we can play one of the three roles: the victim, the villain, or the hero, according to renowned psychologist Dr. Stephen Karpman. If we can control our interpretations, we can control our world.

It's amazing that your mindset determines which of these three roles you choose to play at any given time. Your mind helps you create a self-fulfilling prophecy. When I became the *Win It Minute* guy, it became a self-fulfilling prophecy for me because I liked that image so much and people really resonated with it.

If you think about any situation you are in, you can choose to be the victim, the villain, or the hero. What would everyone normally want to choose? Everyone's going to pick the hero. I don't know too many people who would consciously to choose to be the victim or the villain. We all want to be the hero. I had to make a choice about which role I wanted to play when my son was born. He had a hole in his heart known as VSD, a ventricular septal defect. There was no cure, and he had to have that hole in his heart surgically repaired, meaning open-heart surgery.

And when my wife and I heard that news, it was the second most pivotal moment in my life—the other being the moment that I discussed earlier regarding the Nick Vujicic book after we lost our first baby.

In both instances, I almost succumbed to the frustration, the anger, and thoughts of, "Why us? This isn't fair." Life is not fair and I could have given in to that anger. But instead, I looked at my wife, who was in tears. She was angry and frustrated. For context, my wife is part Italian so she has fiery eyes. I know that when she becomes sick or becomes sad or hurt, she becomes angry. In that moment, I knew she was on that verge of becoming very angry. I knew I had to either decide to go down that road with her, or I could be the hero and assure her it will be all right. That was a conscious choice, and there is no guarantee that choice is easy. It almost never is.

Thus, I had to dive deeper into reading more books, more inspiration, and finding more motivation so I could keep a positive mindset and be the rock for my wife, for my family, and for everyone around us. I had to be the hero in that situation. I couldn't be the victim. There were plenty of people around me who were perfectly willing to play that role.

The difference between a hero and a victim is that a victim believes life happens TO them, whereas a hero believes that life happens FOR them and looks for the seed of opportunity. When you assume that life is about finding and taking advantage of opportunities—even when bad things happen— you get to be the hero. However, if you believe that life happens to you, then you also must believe that you have no control over what happens, and no control over your responses to those events.

Interestingly enough, victims will usually assume the worst possible outcome and spread that negativity to others. They will complain about how they never get a break or that bad things always happen. It's not a constructive way to live your life. We can ALWAYS live to choose how we interpret what happens in our lives.

Is it easy? Absolutely not!

But that's why heroes are heroes. They provide hope because they LIVE in hope.

Not only are there heroes and victims, but, of course, there are villains as well. Villains don't always have to be the bad guys as they are portrayed in movies and television shows. Sometimes we feel like there is a villain in our lives when we are wronged by someone.

And so many times in our lives, if we feel someone has wronged us, we can feel like retaliating. I have friends that I've lost touch with and they may not respond to me. It's easy to become angry at them and then be tempted to not answer their phone call or email because they didn't respond before. Harboring expectations can be dangerous because everyone has expectations of how they should be treated by others.

When those expectations aren't met, people become angry and hurt. There have been many times where I had unfulfilled expectations of others and that led to anger or resentment, and if those emotions go unchecked, it could lead to the temptation to never talk to them again. But then I have to shift my mindset and remember that I have failed others as well in my communication, and I can't ruin a friendship or relationship over my perceived problems.

When I realize this, I back off and then take on the hero mindset again and remember that my friends may not communicate or do what I had expected in the moment. But when push comes to shove, I know that they are always there.

I believe the greatest discovery in our generation is that human beings, by changing their attitudes and their minds, can change the outer aspects of their lives.

It all starts with the choice to respond to emotions, not react to them. Realize that you can control your emotions, you can control your thoughts, and when you do this you make such a big difference in the world. For me, it makes a big difference because I realize that we can choose our responses to events. The input that we allow into our minds—what we are reading or listening to—helps us frame the world. That helps me filter out the negative input more easily and to stay focused on the great things in life. Confidence and happiness come from within, and it is so important to filter out those things that don't serve you.

For example, the small town in Wisconsin where I grew up was a fishing village. There were certain times of the year where a bunch of fishing boats would come in, and the whole area smelled like fish. It was a horrible smell that would overtake the town. Living there, you become desensitized to it and not even notice it anymore. However, when you'd have friends come and visit you, they couldn't stand the smell. But there's a great life lesson in that.

We become desensitized to the great things in our life because they're always there. For example, we have running water. We always have food available to us. We have a cup of coffee every morning, and we begin to take things for granted because we hardly notice them anymore.

By the same token, you realize that you can become desensitized to the negative things and start to notice the positive things more often. One of the most powerful things that you can do in your day is train your mind to see the good in the world and not to see the bad. So many people focus on all the negatives in the world more than they see the good, and there are so many good things coming at us on a daily basis. But most people will filter out the good and see the bad because that's the way they train their brain.

Interestingly enough, the brain is designed to see negative things in the name of "protecting" us. Back in the day, our brains were designed to protect us from saber tooth tigers in the wild, but obviously we're not in the wild anymore. We now understand that we don't have to always be looking for negative things in our environment.

For example, when you are in a coffee shop, the first thing you might notice is the long line. You can choose the negative interpretation of this and believe that waiting a few extra minutes is a bad thing. The alternative would be to see the good in a situation and decide to catch up on messages, or perhaps talk to the person next to you in line and strike up a conversation.

We simply notice the situations that happen and automatically decide that there is a negative outcome on the way. However, the happiest people in the world are those who choose to see the good in every situation. Training our brains to see that positive outcome takes some effort, but it is well worth it.

CHAPTER FOUR

THE WINNING PERSPECTIVE

You were born to win, but to be a winner you must
plan to win, prepare to win, and expect to win."
– Zig Ziglar

Zig Ziglar is one of the most well-known and impactful motivational speakers of our lifetime, and he firmly believed in the power of human potential and achievement. One of his foundational beliefs is he understood that everyone has the potential for greatness, but it doesn't happen randomly. Greatness is only obtained by developing a plan, doing what is necessary to execute that plan, and then having the confidence and belief that what you want is available for you.

It starts with the idea that we are all born to win.

For some people, the idea of being born to win may not resonate. When I was a child, my parents didn't give me a lot of material things, but they gave me everything I truly needed by believing in me and giving me the expectancy that I could do anything. I wasn't the most talented at any one sport, any one skill, or any one thing in life. But anything I did, I worked continually at it, and as a result, I became better at it.

Taking action toward a goal became a habit to me, and I learned that moving forward was the most powerful thing I could do. Being born to win means recognizing that you have everything around you that you really need. Surrounding yourself with people who are supportive and believe in you is the crucial first step to achieving anything.

Preparing to win is also very important because once you identify what you want, you have to prepare yourself for your moment of excellence.

For example, in high school I was very skinny and was not a great athlete. However, I liked sports, so I joined wrestling because my older brother was in that sport. I wasn't great at it, but all my good friends were what I considered unbelievable wrestlers.

However, most of them quit because they weren't reaching the expectations that they wanted to achieve in their perspective.

But I didn't know any better because it was new to me, and I just kept moving forward and was becoming a better wrestler. Even though I was very skinny and wasn't strong by any means, I just used what I had to my advantage. I had a huge reach and I was wrestling in a low weight class—and I used it to my benefit. I didn't even realize it at the time, but I just kept focusing on what was in front of me.

I succeeded even though all my friends who were much more talented than me had quit.

They left the sport, and I just kept moving forward and ended up getting to the top because I had an unshakeable belief in myself and I never gave up. I had the expectation that I was going to win because with anything I've ever done, I've come on top by continuing to move forward. I won conference championships and made it to the state wrestling tournament.

While I didn't win or make the finals, I just kept moving forward. My training partner and good friend at the time was one of the best wrestlers in the state and just by training with him it rose my skill set exponentially as training every day with greatness tends to rub off on you because you have no room for error even in your practice time.

The great lesson for me was to use what I have, and not wish I had what others had. We don't all possess the same skills or talents. At times, it may seem incredibly unfair.

However, life is not fair for anybody, which makes it fair for everybody.

It seems like a paradox, but the truth is that it comes down to our perspectives. When life doesn't seem fair and we are facing obstacles, it's easy to feel frustrated—especially in the early stages of the struggle. But I've always realized that when dealing with obstacles, 10 percent of life is what happens to you and 90 percent is how you react to it. We all face challenges on any given day, but it's all about how you handle it.

Having The Proper Perspective

Perspective is so important.

We tend to take things for granted and don't realize the blessings we have in front of us. As I mentioned, I grew up in a small Wisconsin town. My career has taken me to much larger cities, including Dallas, Texas, and Orlando, Florida, where I currently live.

When I arrived in Dallas, I was enamored by how big everything was. But the people I met who had lived there for many years didn't always appreciate how great it was. They were used to their surroundings, so it was no big deal to them.

I just loved all of the possibilities that were available and chose to take advantage of every opportunity. Not everyone gets to experience a big city, so I appreciated all of the things surrounding me.

Another thing that people tend to take for granted is the birth of a healthy child. As I mentioned, my wife and I lost our first child, and our second child was born with a heart defect.

Life is sometimes very unfair.

Why us?

Why did we have to experience such tremendous challenges in simply HAVING a family, let along raising one?

We may never know the answer to those questions, but again, perspective is critical.

When you are at a hospital, you realize that many people have it far worse than you do.

The second time around, we got to come home with a child. It gave us perspective so that when we came home with our baby, we weren't upset if he was keeping us up all night, had to change a diaper at 3:00am, or couldn't watch Netflix.

All of our other friends that were talking about their favorite TV shows that they got to watch, and complaining about not getting enough sleep as a result made us realize we thought that the greatest blessing was simply being at home.

Just Show Up!

If you want more good fortune in life, if you're looking for your lucky break, then you have to prepare and develop your mindset and skills every day.

I don't believe there is any such thing as pure luck. Showing up and being ready for opportunity is 90 percent of how things happen in life.

For example, all my jobs have come to me simply because I showed up. I was never the best qualified candidate, but because I had shown up and met somebody prior to the interview, there was always a key influencer who helped make the decision. People decide to work with you or hire you for a job, and making a solid first impression is critical. Those decisions are all made when you're not in the room.

This first impression may have been when that person met you three years prior, and they remember that you were an outgoing, positive person and that made it easier to remember who you are. And then three years later they have an opportunity to hire you. Always have your best face on at every opportunity. Sometimes we don't feel like putting on our best face, but whether you realize it or not, someone is always watching.

Have A Consistent Morning Routine

The best way to plan to win, prepare to win, and expect to win is to have a consistent and powerful morning routine to set your day on fire.

For me, it starts with getting up at 5:30am.

I jump out of bed and I cannot wait for that first sip of coffee because it energizes and fuels me. While I'm doing that, I'll read inspirational articles, whether it's based on motivation or psychology, to set my mind right so that I'm prepared for the entire day.

I don't read the newspaper or watch news programs on television because I found that I operate so much better when I feed positive ideas into my head instead of the negativity that is so prevalent in the news.

It's up to you to program your own mind. If you don't, then others will program it for you—and the results of that programming will probably not benefit you.

If you are looking for great examples of what you should be reading, I recommend Zig Ziglar, Tony Robbins, Jim Rohn, or Les Brown.

My morning routine continues with me spending some time reading an inspirational book or something that will contribute to my mindset or my business.

My whole routine takes about 90 minutes each day. By the time I'm done, my kids are up and I'm ready to greet the day.

Or if I happen to be traveling, I'm ready to go to my first business meeting of the day.

I'm grateful for the opportunity to set my mind right first thing in the morning, and because of that, my brain is prepared to think in a certain way no matter what types of obstacles or fires come my way.

We need that type of preparation every day to face whatever is about to happen.

Life rarely unfolds the way we envision it.

We might have a difficult conversation with someone, have a car accident, get stuck in traffic, or have to endure that one person at the office who annoys everyone. Having the right mindset prepared in advance is the secret weapon you get to sharpen every single day—and that's your choice.

If you didn't prepare yourself with that shield of armor with your mindset, then you can go down in flames quickly and that one little obstacle can put you on the wrong path because you didn't set yourself up for success in the morning.

You have the beautiful choice every morning to plan to win, prepare to win, and expect to win as Zig Ziglar so eloquently says.

What choice will you make today?

The ball is in your court.

Take your shot wisely.

CHAPTER
FIVE

THE ATTITUDE OF GRATITUDE WINS THE DAY

We talked about setting up your day for success. Another important component to experiencing the results you want involves having an attitude of gratitude.

According to author Michael Hyatt, a great way to practically apply this principle is to change one word in your life and realize you "get to" do something instead of "have to".

This is really powerful.

"I get the opportunity to watch my kid today", not "I have to watch my kid".

"I get the opportunity to go to work", not "I have to go to work".

Having that mindset encourages me to be thankful for everything that I have in my day, and it will do the same for you.

My beloved mother-in-law Linda always said that if we all sat around a table and shoved our problems to the middle, we would quickly grab our own problems back instead of anyone else's. At that point, we realize that there are much bigger problems out there.

Consider that many people who live in the United States, the wealthiest country in the world, make a good living—some make a *great* living. But many more seem to struggle mightily.

How is this possible in a land of such tremendous opportunity?

Gratitude has a lot to do with it.

There are many examples of immigrants who come to the United States from other lands, and the thing they want most is to have the opportunities that they didn't have elsewhere. Many of them work very hard and become millionaires.

Why do these people succeed with the same opportunities surrounding them, whereas many Americans experience very different results?

I believe these immigrants are happy and grateful to have access to opportunities and they don't take them for granted. The danger of taking things for granted is that there is a temptation to think the opportunity will always be available. That breeds complacency. When complacency sets in, we don't challenge ourselves. Instead, we develop a sense of entitlement.

Entitlement and success are on opposite sides of the spectrum. When we feel entitled, we don't have the motivation to work as hard as we should.

A lack of gratitude is where the spiral begins.

I'm very grateful for the opportunities and challenges that come my way because it gives me a chance to become a better version of myself. If something doesn't go my way, it's simply a chance to learn a new skill or new way of thinking.

That is a huge gift, and successful people understand this.

In contrast, many people ask themselves, "Why me? This is so unfair".

But think about this. My mindset is that I want to find a way through the challenge. There is always something better on the other side of it. Tony Robbins is famous for asking, "What's great about this?" The kneejerk reaction would be that *nothing* is good about this terrible circumstance. However, I have survived 100% of my bad circumstances in life so far, and I know that I am in a much better place than I was 5, 10, or even 20 years ago. I wouldn't ever go back. Going through those obstacles has made me who I am today, and I am *grateful* for that.

In fact, highly successful people *embrace* adversity.

As an example, my wife used to love watching *Grey's Anatomy* and I would watch it with her. I wasn't necessarily a fan of the show, but I would just watch it because she liked to watch it.

If you have never seen it, it's about a bunch of surgeons in a hospital, and the thing that struck me was they were always jockeying for position to be part of an upcoming surgery. The funny thing is, most people do whatever they can to avoid extra work, yet these surgeons *wanted* the extra work because they knew it would make them better at their craft.

They didn't run away from adversity—they ran toward it.

And they were grateful for it! We should all face our jobs and our lives with the same level of enthusiasm!

Another terrific example of someone overcoming adversity is Richard Branson. He had dyslexia while growing up, so he had challenges with reading. That might seem like a bad thing, but it forced him to make friends with the smartest people in class so he could learn from them.

He said that ended up being the greatest gift that he ever received because it taught him how to negotiate and connect with almost any human being and build relationships. That was the biggest skill set that helped him become successful and reach multi-billionaire status.

If you can negotiate and connect with anybody and build relationships with them, you will go far in life.

He had to learn those skills because he believed he was at a disadvantage—and he was so thankful for it.

This is the best time ever to be alive!

Right now, we have the highest quality of life and the highest life expectancy ever on this planet.

Yet we, as a society, spend the majority of our time being frustrated and unhappy.

If our WiFi connection is slow, we get frustrated and angry, not realizing how great of a life that we have.

First world problems, right?

Having perspective is important as 99.9% of human beings to ever walk the Earth would gladly trade places with you at this very moment. Can you imagine if some of the greatest inventors in world history were alive *today?*

Think about the amazing things that could happen if they were with us right now.

As you ponder everything you have going for you, notice how many of those things are absolutely amazing! I would encourage you to make a gratitude list and review it multiple times a day.

Staying focused on the blessings in your life on a continual basis is how you win the day—every day. Even when we face obstacles, remember that you get refined by going through the fire.

You wouldn't be who you are right now without going through the trials and tribulations that have come your way.

Sometimes those challenges get resolved fairly quickly, and other times they represent a thorn in our side that sticks around for a while.

That's where the ability to persevere is required—and that's the subject of the next chapter.

CHAPTER SIX

PERSEVERANCE IS A GIFT

One of my favorite mantras from author Eric Butterworth is "Don't go through life, GROW through life".

In the last chapter, I talked about how we need to be thankful when difficult things come up. We will all experience trials and tribulations as we go through life, so why not *grow* through life as well?

After all, perseverance makes us stronger as we navigate through our challenges successfully.

Walt Disney is a fantastic example of someone who went through the fire before experiencing his biggest victory. We all know he is famous for creating what became perhaps the biggest entertainment empire in the world—but it almost never happened.

In fact, at one point in his life he faced bankruptcy and went through a deep dark depression. His first creation was a rabbit, and it was stolen from him by someone he trusted.

He was on a train traveling when he learned about this loss of his first major cartoon creation.

Imagine this: Walt was prepared to sign a multi-million dollar contract in New York, only to discover that a trusted friend had destroyed his dream by stealing his creation. He was faced with the very real possibility of telling his employees that the company was now bankrupt.

During his three-day train ride, in the midst of his depression, he stared doodling. During those doodling sessions, he came up with the prototype for his most famous character, Mickey Mouse.

Great things can happen when you decide not to give up. When facing your greatest adversity, assess your options, pick the best one, and get started.

Magical things can happen when you open your mind to the creative process.

Another great example involves teaching my kids how to swim. As parents, we enjoy teaching them new skills even though they (sometimes literally) kick and scream the whole way. Of course, they were anxious about it at first—the fear of drowning is real—but the more they were in the water and learned new things, the more they actually began to enjoy it. As they learned to enjoy it, they wanted to hang around for longer periods of time, and then began to make new friends. So many great things happened for them because they overcame their fears and doubts.

It was all about getting past the initial trepidation and moving forward.

I'll never forget when my daughter, Addison, was ten months old and she was experiencing her first swimming lesson. We enrolled her in swimming because we knew that it would teach her valuable lifesaving skills.

However, the whole experience taught *me* even more valuable lessons about the power of never giving up and persisting through challenges as if your life depended upon it. As my infant daughter was tossed into the pool and her head was pushed under water, she had no choice but to try and stay afloat. In between her screaming and crying, she had to learn to stop crying so she could catch her breath when she popped her head above water. When her head was above water, she could either cry or grasp for breath. Eventually, she learned that crying was working against her, so she chose to grab her breath rather than cry.

How often in life do we, as adults, face obstacles and then decide to focus on the barriers and negative things? How often do we complain or sulk instead of deciding to simply breathe and keep swimming forward toward our goal?

Every challenge we face can be viewed as an opportunity to learn, however we must be better aware of what we are teaching ourselves. Parenting, much like business, is all about the mindset of "just keep swimming". When my first child was born, I had no idea how to be a father or a husband to a wife with a newborn. We read many books and took classes on how to be parents, but ultimately, the only real teacher we had was experience. By the time our third child was born we were not reading books on parenting three children, we were just learning from the act and experience naturally kicked in.

This is how any great business person or entrepreneur succeeds as well. You can read all the books you want, take a class, or whatever you feel is going to teach you how to succeed in business. But ultimately, one of the greatest teachers is experience and the mindset of just keep swimming.

Nobody is born an expert at anything. We all had to learn to crawl, walk, ride a bike, find a date, start a business, earn a living, and breathe. Think about it—you don't think twice driving down the freeway, you just do it out of instinct.

Everything in life that is worthwhile makes you uncomfortable at first. Starting a business, parenting, loving someone, and starting a diet are all hard at first. How many people give up when anything they are trying to accomplish gets tough or uncomfortable? However, if you ask any successful business person, they will tell you the number one reason they succeeded was because they didn't give up and just kept swimming.

Yes, asking for someone's business or asking somebody out on a date is tough because they could reject you. But what if they say yes? Then the work actually just begins. You still have to work at everything to be successful, but if you just keep swimming and don't cry you will find it is a lot easier to breathe than if you are letting your frustrations take the place of soaking in breaths of oxygen that allow you to stay afloat.

My daughter Addison taught me the power of staying afloat as she had no choice but to stop crying and fight to stay above water, and then before she knew it, she was back in my arms wrapped in a towel looking up at me smiling. She was proud of her accomplishment and I was proud of her.

What could you accomplish today if you vowed to keep your head above water and decided to just keep swimming and moving forward no matter what obstacle you faced? Now, most of the problems we face in our daily lives are not life or death, and that makes them so easy to quit when they make you uncomfortable. You could simply binge on a series on

Netflix, play that new video game, or break your diet for that instant gratification. Is it worth putting off your next breath and stop swimming upstream so you can just stay where you are or are you willing to keep moving forward, and just keep swimming?

Life is meant to be lived, and anything worth accomplishing you need to swim upstream for. You are born with all the necessary tools to survive and thrive, but you have to make the choice to do so. You are not faced with many hard choices in your day that make you choose between living and dying, but how often do you choose the easier path when the harder path of continuing to swim leads to a better life?

Sometimes we can learn a lot from others, especially children. At times, they can be absolutely fearless and are willing to try anything, and at other times, it takes a while. As adults, however, we tend to be more cautious. We imagine the worst-case scenarios coming true, even though they often don't. This prohibits us from even trying, when in fact, the thing we are afraid of could end up becoming the biggest blessing we can imagine.

Just like my kids learning to swim and actually beginning to love it, we can experience the same thing as adults.

My kids have their mother and me to challenge them as they encounter new situations, but as adults we don't always allow others to challenge us in the same way.

We encourage our kids to try something new every day, but as adults are we willing to do this? If we don't *have to,* we don't want to. And when we don't try new things or allow ourselves to be stretched to expand our horizons, we lose opportunities to persevere.

Perseverance is a gift.

In business, it can take a long time for a new venture to generate income or become successful. If you are committed to your goal, you will find a way.

Sometimes, life tests us to see how badly we really want something. That means *not* giving up when things get tough. Our challenges represent an opportunity to pivot to something more productive.

Thomas Edison very famously attempted to invent the light bulb 10,000 times before finding the solution. His perspective was illuminating though, in that he didn't consider any of those previous attempts to be failures. Instead, he simply viewed it as 10,000 ways that didn't work.

How many of us would give up after failing that many times?

Most of us might try something fewer than 10 times, and sadly, a lot of people give up after trying *once*.

You can't expect to have long-term success if you think that you will hit the jackpot after only one attempt. Certainly, a blind squirrel can find a nut from time to time on its first try, but it is a rare circumstance.

What situations are you facing where you are sorely tempted to give up? Before doing that, look for people who have succeeded where you have previously failed, then learn how they overcame their struggles.

Perseverance can be the greatest gift you can ever receive. It will make you stronger, more resilient, and even happier.

Why?

Because you have the chance to prove to yourself that if you can get through *this* situation, you can get through anything.

That's a beautiful outcome—and great results are available to you as well.

As long as you don't give up.

Mental toughness is like a muscle, it needs to be worked to grow and develop. Developing any skill or learning to swim comes down to your habits.

Are you doing the things you know you're supposed to do on a more consistent basis?

That's the magic question, and only you can answer it for yourself.

CHAPTER
SEVEN

THE SECRET TO SUCCESS IS NO SECRET AT ALL

Your outlook on life is something that is uniquely yours, and it's a choice you get to make every day. It's very simple. You can choose to be a winner or a whiner.

Winners know that they need to take 100% responsibility for everything that happens to them, while whiners look to blame others for everything that happens.

There's a clear distinction.

In sports, for example, the highly successful people know that it wasn't the bad call at the end of the game that prevented them from winning. A lot of things happened during a game that led to the final moment, and if things had been handled differently earlier in the game, that final moment wouldn't have needed to unfold that way at all.

Winning is a team sport, and it rarely happens in a vacuum. More importantly, having the *right* team around you is critical. For example, Michael Jordan is considered by many to be the greatest basketball player to ever play the game. And yet, he didn't start winning NBA titles until Scottie Pippen and few other key players joined his team. As great as Michael was, he needed great teammates, and he need to trust them to do what they do best so that everyone together could achieve more. Often times, winning involves sacrifice. No one can reach the top alone. That frequently involves suppressing one's own glory for the sake of the team's victory.

Choosing to win extends into all areas of life, not just team sports. As NBA Hall of Famer Bill Walton famously said about Michael Jordan, his success was no secret at all as much as it was a choice. The choice to put winning above everything else including his own personal stats.

Marriage is yet another great example of this. At one point in my life, I was a wedding officiant and I got to meet a lot of couples who were getting ready to tie the knot. One theme that came up over and over again—and has even in my own marriage—is that loving each other above all else is a priority. Choosing to win in marriage is about putting your spouse above yourself. Too many people are in the game of life to serve themselves instead of someone else.

That means you aren't right all the time, and it also means that very few things happen at our convenience. Again, sacrifice is necessary as it's more important to get things right in your relationship than it is to *be* right.

Choosing to win is also about creating the life you want.

Winners create.

How do you do that? If you've seen the movie *The Secret*, you already know that there is three-part process to this, which is to ask, believe, and receive. But you also have to put action behind those things and believe that God will provide the way.

To get anything you want in life, you have to ask for it. If you expect something amazing to drop into your lap, you might wait a very long time. Creation is a deliberate process.

Remember, you get to *choose* what you want! If you could have anything in life, what would it be?

Do you want to make $1 million a year? Have six-pack abs? Meet your soulmate? All of these things are possible, but only if you ask first.

The second step is to believe. You have to know deep down that you are worthy of having the thing you are asking for. If you are lacking in belief, then get around people who have achieved what you want. People who have achieved greatness aren't any more special than you are. They've simply figured out a few things faster—that's all!

Then finally, receive. That sounds simple enough, but sometimes when the thing we ask for arrives, we don't recognize it because we were expecting it to arrive within a certain timeframe or in a particular way. Ultimately, God always delivers on time and in the perfect way.

So, the secret to success is not really a secret at all as much as it is a choice.

You get to choose what you want, you get to create it, and along with that comes the responsibility for how it all turns out. It's a lot better than playing the victim card and expecting things to magically turn out for the best.

Life doesn't work that way.

But when you decide what you want and take steps to create it, there's magic to it all.

What do you want to create right now?

It's time to WIN THE DAY!

CHAPTER EIGHT

DESIRE DIFFICULTIES TO WIN THE DAY

Earlier, I talked about how we need to view every problem as a gift. Without problems we would not grow because these can force you to learn new things to make you better.

Previously, we discussed the example of Richard Branson and his problems with dyslexia. We also talked about my son's heart surgery.

My firstborn son Adrian's heart surgery was a pivotal turning point in my journey as a parent. When your eight-month-old baby has a hole in his heart and requires open-heart surgery to repair a VSD, your perspective changes and you are never the same again.

And I thank God every day that I went through that challenge, because it changed my life.

In fact, that's where The Win It Minute was born.

Nowadays, I treasure just throwing a baseball with him rather than wanting him to throw it perfectly like other dads. Sometimes I see other parents wanting their four-year-old kids to throw the ball with the proper form. I just love having the opportunity to simply throw a baseball with him.

It's amazing how a mindset shift can change your perspective. I have a philosophy that I *get* to throw baseballs with my kid, rather than think I have to.

Going through a tragic moment is life-changing for all of us. In that moment, it felt like the worst thing that could have ever happened. But realistically, it's a blessing in disguise because you get that mindset shift as a gift.

When I was a kid we grew up modestly. We didn't come from money, but I still had a happy childhood. Many of my friends had more opportunities than I did because their families had more money. They had everything that you could dream of, so it seemed.

My advantage, however, is that I developed a strong work ethic and a stronger mindset. While I didn't have the same luxuries or have certain doors open up for me as a youth, I'm stronger because of that today.

And I appreciate everything I have. I don't feel entitled, and I feel grateful for everything. That is so important, because we can be much happier when we focus on what we are grateful for—and even more importantly, when we focus on the great lessons that our current situations are teaching us.

Here's a radical mind shift. What if you viewed your challenges as *desirable*? That can completely alter your mindset.

Did I want my child to go through his health challenges? Not at all! But when we choose to view those challenges as opportunities to grow and learn new things about ourselves and about the world in general, we become a better version of ourselves day by day.

Maslow's Hierarchy Of Needs is an idea in psychology from Abraham Maslow. This is a theory comprising a five-tier pyramid of needs, where the bottom of the pyramid is the most foundational and the tip of the pyramid is the ultimate goal.

Those five needs in order are physiological, safety, love and belonging, esteem, and self-actualization. The physiological needs have to do with health, housing and other basic needs being met.

Many of us take these foundational needs for granted.

Many of us have our health, and it's easy to move through life without thinking about it. A lot of us have shelter—unless we suddenly find ourselves homeless, we don't think much about that, either.

We may have health and shelter, but what if that shelter is not in a safe neighborhood? That's also a problem.

I could move through all five levels of Maslow's pyramid, but I think you get the point.

At whatever level of needs we are trying to fulfill in our lives, there are struggles that are unique to that part of the journey.

And I think it's very important to go through struggles and meet those challenges in life and your business. That's what enables us to become stronger because that's what really develops us.

For me, working on myself is very important. I had a great opportunity to focus on that aspect of my journey after I moved to Florida.

I had a girlfriend and ended up moving in with her, but that didn't work out. I found myself in a new city by myself and I knew nobody. Well, my newfound free time is what led me to start reading self-help books by Tony Robbins, Zig Ziglar, and others in an effort to develop myself further.

And it really led me down this path that led me to where I am today. That chain of events moved me down a path that ultimately changed my life. It felt like I was experiencing a personal disaster. I had many dark days, but it ultimately led to a new life.

Personal development provided a new focus, and it forced me to find new strengths. It led me down a path of reading motivational and inspirational books. It shifted my mindset because I was content with moving to Florida and having a girlfriend come with me, living in a new place, and having a new job.

After those things were lost, I went through a personal challenge that forced me to become a different person. It ultimately helped me to become a different but better person, which then helped me to find my wife, a new job, an MBA, a whole new set of friends—everything.

It changed my life completely. I was shaken from my contentment and complacency. And I thank God every day for that challenge because I wouldn't be who I am today without that set of challenges. That shifted my mindset.

We all face the choice every single day to view our challenges as circumstances that lead to empowerment instead of victimhood. Either you will wither from a challenge of an obstacle, or you rise up and become better from it.

It's similar to working out. If you're exercising regularly, your body goes through challenges. Each new level of physical challenge you put yourself through eventually makes you stronger.

When you face difficult trials, desire them!

Not just the circumstances themselves, but the end result of persevering through the fire.

Your interpretation of what is going on around you is a *choice*.

Are you seeing your current situation as a nuisance?

Or are you seeing it as an opportunity?

Your choice determines whether or not you win the day.

Make *today* your winning day.

CHAPTER
NINE

POSITIVE THINKING WILL NOT ALLOW YOU TO DO ANYTHING OR EVERYTHING

One of my favorite quotes is from the great Zig Ziglar:

"Positive thinking will not allow you to do anything, but it will let you do everything better than negative thinking."

I love this quote because it illustrates such an important concept. Many people don't put a lot of stock into the idea of positive thinking because they don't do much of it.

It's natural to minimize something we don't understand or practice on a regular basis. A lot of the same people don't believe that the Law Of Attraction is real—they think it sounds nice in theory, but not terribly practical.

Standing on its own, they're right.

The missing piece to it all is *taking action*. The Law Of Attraction states that when you ask for something, and you believe it to your very core, then you will receive it.

Notice that taking action isn't explicitly stated.

Positive thinking—without action— won't allow you to do anything you want in this world. However, having a positive mindset combined with taking massive action will allow you to do everything better.

Scientific studies show that when you're in a positive or happy mood, your brain is firing on all cylinders. You're more apt to be more successful when you have positive, successful thoughts.

The belief that things are possible is the greatest gift that we can have. This has applications in a lot of areas. Let's look at sales for example. If someone believes that they are about to make a sale, they will be more likely to follow up on their leads and not give up. And it's because they believe it's possible.

However, if that salesperson doesn't think that a sale is possible, they'll give up shortly after they make their pitch. The pure belief that it's possible gives them the best chance at success.

Following up is the most important aspect of any business transaction. People will follow up more often if they believe that there's an opportunity for success.

I see this a lot, even with my kids. As a parent, you learn a lot in life by watching and observing your kids. For example, when my kids learned how to ride a bike, they started with the belief that it was possible. They saw their friends riding bikes, so they believed that if their friends could ride a bike, they could as well. They don't know any differently. The concept of impossible is foreign to them. If they hopped on the bike and fell down, it never discouraged them from the idea that eventually they would succeed. They keep going after it.

They don't think there's an alternative view that they wouldn't successfully ride their bike. That's not even a thought process of theirs.

As adults, however we don't always have that same unwavering belief.

Why is that?

I believe it's because we see the world not as it is, but as we are. It's through our very own lens that we see others and the world. People who doubt positive thinking do so out of fear.

If you accept the results you have gotten before, then you never have to face fear.

But please don't limit others.

It's so easy to project limits onto others if we give in to our self-perceived limitations. We tend to do this a lot, whether it's with our kids, our co-workers, or anyone else.

All of us deal with self-limiting beliefs in different areas of our lives. But we should project optimism to everyone so that they can reach higher. Belief that anything is possible is a gift.

Any salesperson knows if they don't have a shot at landing a deal, they won't even bother making the call. That leads to a sale not being earned. But if you think you have a shot, you make the call, and then you make the follow up call, and then the one after that.

All of us want to accomplish something significant. We want to write a book, we want to start a new business, or even get in shape and run a 5K. But when we see the first obstacle, we give up.

If we had the same mindset as kids who don't see the prospect of failure quite so easily, I think we would all accomplish a lot more in our lives and in our businesses.

Sports is another terrific area where we see positive thinking make a difference in performance.

Let's look at basketball for example.

If LeBron James walks up to you as you are about to shoot two free throws with the game on the line and says to you, "You'll never make that shot, you're not good enough," how would that make you feel?

On the flip side of the coin, if LeBron walks up to you and says he believes in you and you're going to nail this free throw to win the game, don't you think you have a significantly higher chance at making it? If LeBron James said anything like that to me I would run through a wall with confidence.

Positive thinking will definitely allow you to do things better than not believing in yourself at all.

I use basketball as an example because I love the game. I used to play basketball with a group of guys once a week. On one specific occasion, one of the guys actually wore a Fitbit. At the end of the game he said, "Hey guys, did you realize that we just ran nine miles?"

I thought to myself, "Wow, I ran nine miles. I've never done that before!" But if you asked me to run five miles with you today, it would seem like such an insurmountable goal. I'm sure that if I was just running by myself, I'd probably give up after three or four miles.

The idea that I was having fun and not focused on running nine miles is what made it happen. I was enjoying the process and engaging in a fun activity with my friends.

I was enjoying the process.

I believe the same phenomenon translates to business as well. Entrepreneurs love to build and create things. It's all about having the positive belief that what you are doing is making a difference, and also about having fun along the way. The most successful entrepreneurs know that no matter what happens, there is always a way to turn something into a good thing.

I've forged ahead with so many business opportunities because I've believed it's possible. The belief of that possibility is the most important aspect. I've been told so many times that it wasn't a smart move to move forward in something, but I knew in my gut that I was onto something great.

Sometimes, you have to be smart enough to not quit.

When I first moved to Florida, I was trying to make friends and build connections. During this time, I also decided to pursue my MBA from a local university. When I showed up, it was an MBA program for executives and it happened to be at the exact same time that NASA was preparing to decommission. Essentially, the government was shutting down NASA, so this MBA program had a bunch of rocket scientists who were about to be out of a job.

So, what are they doing? They were also pursuing their MBA.

I knew the competition in this program would be fierce.

I showed up for my first class, and there were 32 people in my class, and 24 of them were NASA rocket scientists. This would be a 19-month program with the same students.

That was really intimidating. In fact, I wanted to quit after the first week. I knew I was in way over my head. However, I forged ahead because I had a positive mindset.

In fact, on the first day, I met someone in the class who turned out to be a sports fan like I was. So, I started talking about sports with him and I realized that even though he was a rocket scientist and absolutely brilliant, he was still a human being.

And the way I was able to connect with him over sports made me look at all of them differently. I didn't quit the MBA program and I ended up learning so many skills from the rocket scientists.

This whole experience actually led me down an amazing path because I realized that we could relate on a lot of levels even though I perceived that they were so much smarter and had a much higher level of technical expertise than I did.

They weren't "better" than I was, we simply had different skill sets. They knew all about statistical analysis whereas I didn't quite so much. On the flip side, they hated presenting in front of the class but I thrived on it. They didn't enjoy talking to people or presenting their results in front of the room.

I saw that as a strength of mine.

When you realize that we are all gifted differently and that no one is inherently "better" than anyone else, you will be a lot happier. Comparisons can be toxic because we naturally gravitate to negative thoughts.

You don't have to be the smartest person in the room. Once you realize what your unique gifts are and you decide to dwell in those gifts continuously, you will be happier and, as a result, you will make a greater impact on the world.

Discovering my gift for presenting in front of groups helped me make friends in my MBA program because these rocket scientists hated doing something that I loved. I became the de facto presenter for our groups and people started to like my presentations.

That was one of the things that eventually led me to the Win It Minute. To this day, I'm still friends with these guys, and they'll watch a Win It Minute and tell me how much they love it. That fuels me to keep doing it, and it gives me positive affirmation.

And I discovered this gift because I kept a positive mindset and continued moving forward. The initial obstacle of feeling intimidated almost led me to quit the program one week into it, but I resolved to find connections. People with a positive mindset will find a way to make their situations better in any way they can.

I didn't let my initial negative mindset dominate.

I quickly overcame it and because I kept moving forward and had a positive mindset, it led me down this amazing path for me to discover my strengths. In turn, that has led me to so many business successes and business opportunities, and led me into some of the best roles that I've ever had.

I also believe I discovered my strengths and built a positive attitude because I was willing to have my limits stretched.

That's what being in the MBA program did for me.

In nature, if you think about an oak tree, it will only grow so big if you plant it in a pot. That tree can't outgrow its current environment. Once the roots fill the pot, it won't grow any further.

The problem isn't the tree, it's the environment.

But once you replant that tree outside, it has much more room to grow—not only because there is a lot more space in which to grow, but because now the tree has the opportunity to battle the elements and get stronger.

Notice that I used the phrase "opportunity to battle the elements". That's a mindset shift. Most people would say they *have* to go through the battles.

But when you view growth as something you *get* to do instead of something you *have* to go through, it completely changes the way you view it.

How are you viewing your current challenges?

Do you *get* to encounter them, or do you *have* to battle them?

Remember, positive thinking will not allow you to do anything or everything. However, it requires that you take action in the right direction.

You choose your thoughts and you choose your actions. The attitude and choices you make today will impact the results you get in the future.

Choose wisely.

It only takes a minute to win it.

CHAPTER
TEN

ABC - ALWAYS BE CURIOUS

"If you do what you've always done, you'll
get what you've always gotten."
– Tony Robbins

As humans, we are creatures of habit. We get into familiar routines that we believe serve us. We find ways of doing things that work well for us. However, it's easy to relax and then those habits put us in a rut.

We begin to live life on autopilot and do these things without thinking about it anymore, and as a result, we lose our curiosity.

Sometimes, it's necessary to change things up and explore new and better ways of accomplishing our objectives.

That involves cultivating a sense of inquisitiveness.

Failure to do this regularly can lead to stagnation and dullness. We don't grow when we are in state of stagnation.

Exposing ourselves to different ways of doing and thinking can broaden our horizons in unimaginable ways.

I once read that 78% of people in America don't move farther than 15 miles from the homes they grew up in. That means most Americans are following similar traditions and perspectives they learned from their parents, who learned from their parents, and so on. I love tradition and family, but at the same time, I have moved and traveled the country and changed my mind from viewing things in different perspectives and from different viewpoints of others.

I grew up in a small town with less than 10,000 people. Growing up, my parents bought cars and shopped at the same stores their parents did, and you followed a tradition with most everything you did from shopping to following the same sports teams, and getting the same education as everyone else.

If you don't expose yourself to different perspectives, you become consumed with your old beliefs, and without even realizing it, you rarely switch your mindset. We adopt a philosophy or strategy based on simply what we have been exposed to without knowing if it's the optimal way to do things.

There's a Zen Buddhist concept called *shoshin*, which refers to the idea of letting go of your preconceptions and having an attitude of openness when learning something.

Kids learn stuff much faster than we do as adults because they don't have as much of a preconceived notion about things. How many times do we as adults not try something because we don't want to? Nobody is forcing us to try anything now that we are free and living outside our parents' home.

It's easier to entertain the idea of letting go when we invite ourselves to view things from a different perspective. For example, when you are flying in an airplane 10,000 feet in the air, you literally view the world differently than you do while on the ground.

When you're single and don't have kids, you view life differently than you do once you have a spouse and children. Before my three kids were born, I had no clue what it took to be a parent or even how to do it. However, several years into this venture, I feel like I am learning every single day, and getting better at it—but I have no choice. I have to learn and grow as a parent because my wife and kids are depending on me to.

In that scenario, you are forced to grow because your new circumstances demand it. But what are you doing in your life to grow and get better at something when you are not forced to? A mind stretched by a new experience can never go back to its old dimensions. This simply means that new thoughts or experiences change our minds and our perspectives.

In fact, each day brings new possibilities if you let them flow into your life with an open mind and open perspective. I have met many people and encountered many ideas over the past few years, many of them through my children. However, I can assure you that even the smallest encounters have changed me because I allow them to by using a different perspective. If my kids are watching Tarzan on TV, I could simply zone out and let it play in the background, or I could watch with childlike wonder and actually see there is a meaning behind every interaction and know that my kids are actually getting a life lesson through the movie. In movies, days and years go by in minutes, and relationships or interactions seem important in the moment...but in our life, someone you meet today could wind up bringing a huge business opportunity to you years from now. How you treat that person or that situation makes all the difference in winning the moment for your future self today!

Children are naturally curious because they enjoy trying new things. For example, I enjoy throwing a baseball around with my son. The better he got at it, the more I wondered how good he could actually get.

I began to fantasize about how he could become a superstar—it's perfectly natural for a dad to think about things like that—so I signed him up for a youth baseball team. Granted, he was three years old at the time, but I was looking forward to watch him grow and develop.

I quickly realized that he wasn't as skilled as a lot of the other kids, and he was intimidated.

I knew that he loved to learn and still does, but he felt inadequate among the older kids on the team and wanted to quit.

I knew that he still loved baseball and he wanted to learn more about it, so I didn't let him quit. It just took more time for him to play. He was only three, so I would still go out in the backyard with him and play baseball with him. Slowly but surely, he began to learn more and more. Then the next time I signed him up to play, he was the best player on the team because I didn't give up on teaching him and he didn't give up on learning.

Great things can happen when you keep your thirst for learning alive. I think the most important thing that we can do in our daily lives is to realize that you can never stop learning.

So many people stop that learning process. Once they get into a groove in their life, they just coast through it and they're not always open to learning new things.

People become creatures of their own habits and follow a similar path day in and day out.

In one of my Win It Minute videos, I talked about how we sometimes have the Popeye mentality—I am what I am. Their mindset is that they can't change because "this" is how they were made.

Well, there's no greater fallacy in the world.

Our brain is actually hardwired to adapt to change. As human beings, we're constantly looking for new opportunities. Our brains are also hardwired to protect us. And the best way to protect us is to avoid changes in our environment. So many people don't change their environment, but learning is the biggest tool for changing them.

The average adult reads less than one book a year, but the average successful executive reads 34 books a year. The average adult watches 3.5 hours of TV a day, whereas the average successful executive watches less than 20 minutes of TV a day. This is what can happen when we lose a thirst for learning after we finish school.

My first Win It Minute video wasn't nearly as good as my 100th video, but I kept going and kept learning. The content got better as I continued learning new things on my journey because that's what I share. I watch the first one now and again, and I'm almost embarrassed by it because I am so much better at it now than I was then. But we all have to start somewhere, and I wouldn't trade that first one for anything in the world.

And I've learned more creating these Win It Minute videos every day than I did from my $50,000 MBA when I was studying with rocket scientists. I learned more about myself, and I've learned incredibly more by going down this path, not only on what it takes to be successful in life by reading so many books and articles, and looking for the inspiration, but from the people that I've met along the way.

The thirst for learning has made me a better and more successful person. When we maintain that curiosity on a daily basis, it moves us forward and helps us expand into our greatness.

CHAPTER ELEVEN

SUCCESS IN LIFE IS FIGURE-OUT-ABLE

"Your attitude, not your aptitude, will determine
the altitude you soar in life."
– Zig Ziglar

A famous basketball star was once asked what the secret to success is. His answer was profound. "Ultimately, the secret to success is not a secret at all as much as it is a choice, the choice to be a winner above all else". What he meant was there is no blueprint to success in any endeavor, it is something you have to work at and figure out as you go, but the most important thing is to keep a strong mindset and keep working at it.

I have found that the key to life is not stopping at the first roadblock, but realizing that everything is "Figure-Out-able". What this means is that you have to simply keep trying and adapting your approach at things and eventually you will overcome it—but the key is not to give up.

Think about it. We have all encountered moments where we didn't know what to do so we had to figure it out. When we were children and couldn't talk yet, we had to figure out how to communicate what we wanted to our parents. It meant pointing or looking intently at something, or perhaps making a sound that indicated what we needed at the moment.

Children have an amazing ability to be curious and adaptable to situations. As adults, we sometimes forget that. The most successful people in life are those who consistently remember and apply that principle. You either figure it out or you give up.

But here's the key.

Everything is "Figure-Out-able".

In Tony Robbins' book, *Awaken the Giant Within*, he talks about life metaphors. One of my favorite ones that he uses as an example is this:

Life is like a Jeopardy game. All of the answers are on the board, but the winner is the one who comes up with the right questions.

That is such an empowering way to view things. That presupposes that there is an answer to every challenge.

Thomas Edison certainly believed this. As I mentioned earlier, when he was trying to invent the light bulb, he failed 10,000 times before finding the right solution, and he documented everything he did so that he wouldn't make the same mistake again. Interestingly, he didn't view himself as failing 10,000 times. He saw it as 10,000 ways that it didn't work.

How many times are we willing to try something before giving up?

10,000? 1,000? 100?

Or perhaps one? A lot of people give up after their first try, and then they throw their hands in the air and proclaim, "It didn't work, told you!"

How many of those people are world-class successes?

None.

In business, I notice quite often that it isn't the smartest or most educated people who are the most successful. It's the ones that adapt and figure things out.

They see obstacles as opportunities.

I had a really good friend that lived in my neighborhood. He had a great job, he had just bought a new house, he bought a new pool, and his wife was pregnant.

Life was good for him—until there was a business shift at his company. He got laid off.

However, he didn't panic and he didn't get upset. He knew that his job was to find a new job and he figured it out. At his previous job, he spent all day solving problems for other people. Now he was simply solving a big problem for himself,

He applied the mindset of figuring out a solution rather than focusing on the problem. He worked at it, and it wasn't more than a month later that he landed a new job with a new company. It ended up being a better job than the last one and I was so impressed.

It left such an indelible example on me because most people dwell on obstacles and feeling that they'd been wronged, and so they focus on the problem.

But when you focus on the solution, you will always find one. There's a solution to every single problem. But people don't work on that or won't try to figure it out.

Even in my work day, if I have a client that doesn't return my email, I call. Then, if they don't return my call, I FedEx them a letter and that gets their attention. But, if neither of these patiently persistent tactics work then I have to amp it up, and if it's that important I SHOW UP!

80% of life is just showing up and being present. You would be amazed at what you can accomplish when you communicate with people. Again, you can't just take the first NO. It is an opportunity to discover a new path to success.

That's why everything is "Figure-Out-able".

And that's the legacy I want to leave my children. There is a solution to every problem. That's why I started writing blog posts and doing the Win It Minute videos. My goal is to inspire everyone that if there is a question, there is also an answer.

CHAPTER TWELVE

10 WORDS TO CHANGE YOUR LIFE

We've talked about having a positive mindset a lot so far. Your mindset is a direct reflection of the way you perceive what's happening around you. For example, if you have a lot of fear around a virus turning deadly and letting it dramatically affect the way you live life, then that perception will dictate your mindset. However, if you perceive that things aren't as bad as the media wants you to believe, then your mindset will be in a different place.

The bottom line is this:

If we can control our interpretation, we control our world.

The way we view things, the way we interpret our perspective, is shaped by our interpretation. I did a Win It Minute video one time which was about my kids having candy on Easter. My daughter was two years old at the time, and her two older brothers were taking her candy. Of course, she was upset about this.

She struggled to open the wrapper on one of her candies, so I reached down and said, "Here, I'll open it for you."

I tried to grab it from her so I could help her, but because of her previous encounters with her brothers taking candy, she thought I was trying to steal it. So, she threw a fit and ran away from me.

She couldn't open up her candy and wasn't able to eat it because she didn't understand that I was trying to help her. She also didn't see that her interpretation was different than my intent.

I think so many of us do that.

Every single day in business, for example, someone may be trying to help you but you interpret it in a different way. Someone may compliment your shirt and you may wonder if that person is making fun of it.

If you interpret the compliment as a negative, then your perception is coloring your world and you'll look at that person negatively even though they intended to do something nice for you.

This is especially true in relationships.

The success of any message is in the interpretation. For example, if my wife is upset with me because I didn't wash and clean out the car, it can lead to an argument where she's angry with me.

She may not be angry with me because I didn't wash the car, though.

She might be angry with me because she's interpreting that I don't care enough about our relationship to want to take the time to wash the car.

And if I can interpret her message the right way, then I can understand that I have to give her more attention and do what's important to her in that moment. If my reason for not washing and cleaning the car was because I was busy all day with a work event and taking the kids to soccer, then *my* interpretation of the event would be, "How could she be mad at me for not washing the car?" That could lead to negativity and anger back at her.

Every single day we face situations where the way we interpret interactions with other people can set us on a path of two completely different directions. One of these directions can lead to healthy, beneficial, successful relationships, and the other one can lead to negative, unsuccessful relationships.

As Shakespeare once wrote, "There is nothing good or bad in this world, but thinking so makes it so". Every day I see an article come across my Facebook feed on how eating chocolate or drinking wine is the best thing you can do to improve your health today. These articles usually present themselves as revealing the big secret to life.

Well, I am not here to argue with scientific studies like these, but I do know that I love to drink coffee in the morning and the more I drink, the happier I feel. I have started my day with coffee for years now, and it sets up my day for success. When I start drinking the coffee, I get fired up to Win The Day, and I now think coffee is the trigger to set off a Win The Day mentality that has fueled me for the past decade.

It creates momentum for me.

If you love sports like I do, you can see how momentum is the most powerful force on Earth, but especially in sports. There is no exact formula for it, you can't describe it accurately or prescribe it, but when you see it you know it.

I love watching the NBA playoffs for this one simple reason. Regardless of the talent differential at any given moment, you can see momentum swings in the game. It is truly my favorite part to observe when you feel the momentum shifting from one team to the other. The announcers call them "runs," but when a tidal wave of momentum takes over and the crowd is going wild, it is truly a remarkable thing.

The next time you feel the momentum of the day turning on you, do what those million-dollar basketball coaches do. Simply call a timeout and gather yourself.

But I don't have the time in my day to call a timeout.

Well, those coaches call 30-second timeouts periodically throughout the game. Sometimes that's all it takes to suck the momentum out of the other team and get your team back in the right mindset. If it works in professional sports, it can work in your life as well. Once you realize you control your mindset and emotions simply by your interpretation, you control YOUR WORLD!

Get out there and start momentum in your favor. Ride that wave to a successful day. Realize that you are in control of the direction you want your day to go, and if you control your interpretation of events and realize how each event can lead to something better by simply thinking that way, you will be able to create a winning day and ride the MOST powerful force on Earth, which is momentum.

Your day is ruled by your perceptions, your thoughts, and your actions.

If you can control your interpretation you can control your world.

However, too many people get swept up in the emotion and momentum of life and don't use that incredibly powerful force to move them in a positive direction.

Instead, they let it sweep them into a negative mindset, and thus, a losing day.

We live in the greatest time that any human being has ever experienced. Crime rates are at their lowest, life expectancy is at its highest, and overall quality of life is skyrocketing year over year. However, when you watch the news or talk to other people, they are more often than not apt to tell you how bad their day was and it keeps getting worse. They'll say, "First, I got stuck in traffic, then I spilled my coffee, and then I got pulled over for speeding. Today was just the worst day".

Well, you weren't the reason for the traffic jam, you got to enjoy coffee, you're alive, and you didn't get a ticket.

If you don't let the momentum of a rough morning derail your day, you can set yourself up for success.

It's all in your interpretation of what is happening around you.

But it's a *choice.*

Now is your time to Win The Day!

CHAPTER THIRTEEN

SUCCESSFUL PEOPLE CHOOSE TO WIN THE DAY

I read one time that scientists have proven that our brains and our body move to the strongest impressions of our thoughts. This simply means that you move in the direction of your focus in life.

Winning is a choice and it's a habit.

My favorite misquote of all time is by the most famous coach of my favorite football team, the Green Bay Packers—the team that my family and 680,000 other community members have an ownership stake in.

The great Vincent Lombardi once said:
"Winning is a habit. Unfortunately, so is losing."

People often misquote him as to say "Winning is the only thing". But that's not all he said. He noted how important it was to build a habit of winning because if you don't, you build a habit of losing. When you don't keep playing to win, complacency sets in. That's when bad things can happen.

A great example of this happened on January 8th, 2015. I refer to this as the tragedy in Seattle, where my Green Bay Packers had practically punched a ticket to the Super Bowl.

During this game, the unthinkable happened.

They were winning in the NFC championship by 21 points with less than four minutes to go. And they stopped playing to win. Instead, they started playing not to lose.

The psychology of playing to win instead of playing not to lose is very different. When you play to win, you focus on your goals, you stay aggressive, and you aren't worried about what your opponent is trying to do. You are more focused on what *you* can do.

But when you play not to lose, you begin worrying about everything that your opponent is doing and you begin to get very conservative in your approach to the game.

That's what happened to the Packers.

They chose to focus on not losing rather than winning. And in the last few minutes of the game, the Seattle Seahawks ran their two-minute offense, they gambled and played hard in an effort to come from behind. In an unexpected turnaround they scored enough points in the last few minutes in a miraculous comeback to win because Green Bay went into prevent mode and tried not to lose.

The Seattle Seahawks made the choice to win that day, as all successful people do.

And that's the secret to it all—it's a choice.

In life, the secret to success and happiness is that, ultimately, we have to choose to Win The Day from the moment that you get out of bed, pour your first cup of coffee, and take the first sip.

Most experts will tell you right when you wake up to do something to put a smile on your face and choose to have a great day right out of the gate.

Even though I have read over 500 books and listened to countless podcasts and inspirational speakers in the past five years, even the Win It Minute guy wakes up a little groggy and un-optimistic from time to time.

However, I have actually trained my brain to react to a sip of coffee like the caffeinated drug it is. Coffee time for me is the most exciting and fruitful time of the day! I get up extra early no matter where I am and consume two to three cups of Joe while pouring through inspirational articles or blogs on the web. By preparing myself with a bevy of learning experiences and that quiet time before the day hits me, I already feel equipped to take it on regardless of what comes my way.

For me, having my morning coffee activates my happiness and sets my mind in a positive place.

You see, when you believe something, you start to notice it through your subconscious so much more and you start to see it everywhere. Tony Robbins calls it reticular activation.

My wife and I decided at one point to buy a minivan, so we started researching it.

Have you ever noticed that when you start researching a car that you will start to see the exact same car everywhere on the road?

That happened to us.

We saw minivans on the road, at the grocery store, in parking lots—they were everywhere! My subconscious mind was triggered because now my mind was activated toward a specific target, and now I saw minivans all over the place.

Before we looked at getting that minivan, I didn't notice them much at all because they weren't on my radar.

But, once you trigger something in your brain, you notice it all around you. Just like deciding on a car, if you trigger positive thoughts right away in the morning as I talked about a little bit ago, you will notice more positive things happening for you throughout your entire day.

If you do this, you can live the life of the lyrical genius Christopher Wallace, who once said:
"Damn right I like the life I live, because I went from negative to positive."

You may be wondering who is Christopher Wallace. He was better known as the Notorious B.I.G.

Successful people in life know that each day has challenges, but they are ready for them. They overcome those challenges and turn them into opportunities by arming themselves with a great attitude right out of the gate.

If you're doing that every day, then you have no choice but to be positive as there is no need to be bothered by the world. Unsuccessful people let the world and its problems bother them continuously, and every little obstacle or hiccup during the day throws them off.

Do you have a co-worker or friend that immediately tells you about how brutal their drive was, or the line at Starbucks that was out of control? They are letting natural and beautiful life opportunities turn into negative moments and their day starts on the wrong foot. Once that happens, it's harder to shift gears midday than it is to move in a positive direction from that first sip of coffee.

Psychologists have proven that you move to the strongest impression in your mind. If you are thinking about all the little bumps and obstacles, you will view people and your day in a negative fashion. You have 100% control of your thoughts and your mind as that is literally the only thing you can full control.

Your thoughts determine your actions. That determines your habits, which determine who you essentially are.

Thus, if you choose to think positively and have that mindset triggered over your morning cup of coffee when you do encounter your first obstacle of the day, then that obstacle will come and you will be ready to not let it bother you.

If you do find that negative thought affecting your mindset, just rap to yourself:

"Damn right I like the life I live, because I went from Negative to Positive"

"You know very well who you are
Don't let 'em hold you down, reach for the stars
You had a goal, but not that many

Cause you're the only one, I'll give you good and plenty." -
B.I.G.

Make the choice to Win The Day!
It's *always* a choice.

WIN THE DAY THE JACK NICHOLSON WAY

I'm a big Jack Nicholson fan.

If you are a movie fan, you know that he has been in some of the most iconic films ever made, including *One Flew Over The Cuckoo's Nest*, *A Few Good Men*, *The Shining*, *Batman*, and many others.

But one in particular stood out to me because of a line that his character said in the movie, *The Departed*.

"I don't want to be a product of my environment. I want my environment to be a product of me."

This is such a profound statement and one that has led me to live a more inspired life. I have found that whenever I faced an obstacle or needed to make a massive change, it all began with me and the environment I was surrounding myself with. When I first moved to Orlando knowing no one, I wanted to meet new people and live a fulfilling life in an exciting new city. However, a few years went by and I hadn't met many new people as I focused simply on working.

What did I do about it? I remembered my fondest memories of my friends back home were from playing sports together. Thus, I met one guy and we started a softball team together. It completely changed my life. My environment was now one of hard work by day and playing softball at night. My new teammates grew into great friends. As a result, this led to many more new friends and being inspired to meet my wife and living a more fulfilled life.

However, it all started when I decided to change my environment and not let the world I was living in dictate who I was. I see my kids every day start their day in different ways. Life is sometimes like a boomerang and what you send out comes right back to you. This is never more evident than when I see my kids completely change their mindset based on what I am projecting to them. You are a living magnet invariably attracting into your life what you think about most and allowing God to provide.

Our words become the story we tell ourselves and others. For example, very often my kids will wake up in a bad mood, but I have found that with a little work I can change that for them.

However, as adults, who do we have in our lives that help us with attitude adjustments in the morning to help us set up our day for success? Not too many of us have a boss or spouse where if we are cranky with them, they will look at us with compassionate eyes and do their best to turn our mood positive. In fact, it's the opposite.

If you are cranky and rude to someone, most people will reflect that negative energy right back at you and then double down on that with the next person they encounter.

Thus, your negative response to someone can lead to a multiplier effect on others as they share your bad mood.

The best way to combat this is to create your environment and start your day right. Give yourself positive input to start your day, whether it's a book, an inspirational YouTube video, or if you care to check out some "Win It Minute" videos on my website or YouTube!

Giving yourself this built-in advantage gives you an edge and creates an opportunity to influence others in a positive way. Have a quiet place at home or work where you can focus on giving yourself that morning edge. This will equip you to *make the choice* when something challenging happens.

Remember, your environment doesn't make you, you make your environment.

Don't let the story you are telling yourself hold you back. Realize that you have the power to tell your own story every single day as you are the author, not others. Too often, we let negative posts on social media or rants from friends and neighbors cloud our day in negative ways. Our daily choices to influence our environment are not made in the heat of the moment; they are made in our daily practices.

Tom Brady, for example, doesn't succeed because he runs out onto the football field and makes great decisions in the moment. It's quite the opposite. He spends countless hours preparing, watching film, and practicing those exact moments on the practice field. As a result, during an actual game, when he has a mere second or two to make the right choice, he succeeds because of the habits he chose to hone over his lifetime.

You, too, can change your mindset and practice daily rituals of healthy habits that will allow you to make the right decisions to change your environment, and improve your life and others. It all starts with small adjustments and realizing you have the power to control an entire room with your mindset.

You can choose to see the amazing array of great things that happened, and use those things to write your own story and create your own environment for success. The difference is that now you know you are the author of your own story.

When you feel like your environment is being dictated to you, there's your opportunity to seize control.

For example, I travel a lot in my work. If I get stuck in an airport due to a delay, I've learned not to get angry and upset because that doesn't benefit anyone at all. I can't change it, so I roll with it.

I look at it as an opportunity to read a book that helps me to grow my mind.

If I am driving instead of flying, a six-hour drive can seem endless. But I can listen to great podcasts such as *Success Profiles Radio* (one of my favorites) and learn from expert interviews, or even call a friend and catch up with someone that I normally would feel too busy to call. It's a great opportunity to reconnect with someone that I would normally be too busy to talk to during the day.

Sometimes calling people during my drive has rekindled business relationships where new opportunities come about. As a result, those relationships have shifted my income.

Doesn't it just make sense to not be a product of your environment, rather have your environment be a product of you like the legendary Jack Nicholson said. (I would love to have him on the Win it Minute, anyone have a connection?)

Every day I get to set the tone for my day so that I can create the life and business that I want. It's amazing how as humans we have the incredible ability to actually influence and create the environment around us, and instead, many people simply let the environment impact them and put them in a negative mindset.

And then that impacts their entire day.

Allowing the shiny object syndrome to affect you is a way that results in many people letting their days get dictated to them. Starting your day with social media and email—and letting someone else's agenda control you—can negatively affect your day, whereas filling your mind with positive things will impact your day in a much better way.

Scheduling business meetings at the beginning of the day can also be a great way to take control of your life. In fact, I set the tone of a lot of my business meeting by bringing donuts and coffee. Giving has a way of doing that!

Gratitude has a way of doing that also.

Being thankful for what I have sets the mood for my day. Let's say, for example, that I brought donuts and coffee to a meeting we were having. I'm not looking for gratitude to make *myself* feel better, but your choice to be grateful or not will guide how your day goes. If I brought donuts you perhaps didn't like, or if you like creamer with your coffee and I didn't bring any, do you choose to be thankful for what I brought to the table? Or will you be resentful that I brought something you didn't like?

In that moment, you are choosing between being a product of your environment, or having the environment being a product of you.

Which one will you choose in that moment?

Another great example of how we can create our environment is our response to adversity in the workplace. Not long ago, the company I was working for experienced a total implosion of our operating systems and the products we were selling.

We couldn't ship and deliver to our customers for months at a time, and these customers were used to receiving their product every day.

In that scenario, they couldn't receive shipments for three months. It was a total mess and was the worst-case scenario that you ever want to be in as a business manager or even an entrepreneur. But I realized there was nothing I could do to get the product out the door because it was an operation and software inefficiency that was out of my control.

Every day I was receiving angry phone calls from customers. They weren't irate at me, but they were irate at the situation. So, eventually I had to change the environment that they were calling me in because they were looking to yell at me and pick a fight with me.

But I flipped the script. Every time they called me, I would answer with the most enthusiastic greeting they could ever receive. I would say, "Hey Joe, great to hear from you!" They knew that I knew what the problem was and it totally threw them off. It's hard to be angry at someone that is overly enthusiastic to talk to you and happy to see you. It completely disarms them.

Instead of having a bombastic confrontational conversation, they were disarmed and I looked at it as an opportunity to connect with them more. Some of these people were customers that I hadn't talked to in a year because business was running smoothly.

But now they were calling me every other day, so I was growing a relationship with them. I got to know more about their lives, and I used it as an opportunity rather than just to deflect it and let them be angry. I just did it with an over-aggressive amount of enthusiasm, and it was amazing the way that it flipped the script and turned anger into happiness and enjoyment. I ended up having better relationships with my customers. Many of my other team members lost these customers, and they never did business with my team members again because we couldn't deliver our product.

I had a successful outcome because I grew stronger relationships and connections with these people. They knew the situation was out of my control, so they started to feel sorry for me and we worked together to do the best we could to resolve it. I turned it into an opportunity to grow.

Another great example is coaching my four-year-old's soccer team. When you're working with young children and you're trying to get them going in the same direction, you *have* to create the environment. If you let those children dictate or alter your environment, there is no way you can accomplish anything in a soccer game or a soccer practice. Kids will get easily distracted by their surroundings or by one another, so you have to control the environment and you lead them in the same direction.

But how often do we do that in our personal lives?

We frequently let negative forces affect us. People around us may gossip, or we might spend too much time watching the news which focuses mostly on negative things.

Instead of being programmed by our environment, you can choose to feed yourself the right input. You have the opportunity to impact the environment around you with those choices. And if you have the right mindset, you can actually lead it to a positive environment.

So, once again, it's a choice. How will you choose your environment? That's up to you!

THERE'S NO LUCK IN WIN...
THE MYTH OF LUCK

"The meeting of preparation with opportunity
generates the offspring we call luck."
– Tony Robbins

In the "something for nothing" society that we live in, many people tend to look for the free ride. That could include gambling at a casino, betting on sports, or buying lottery tickets. However, the challenge with relying on these activities to get ahead is that it completely depends on outcomes you can't control.

And in those rare instances where you may score big and win, the winning is almost never sustainable.

I simply don't believe in luck because true success comes from putting in effort—which you *can* control—and putting yourself in a position to succeed. You do this by taking action and meeting the right people who can help you achieve the goals you set for yourself.

A great example of this happened to me during a job search years ago. Studies have shown that people who are more social tend to be "luckier". That's because extroverts connect and socialize, and by doing so, they find and attract more opportunities to them. During this particular job search, I had applied for 387 jobs online. I wasn't willing to settle for the first thing I was offered because I had criteria around what I would (and wouldn't) accept.

During this time, I had also been nurturing my network in hopes of finding something that was close to what I really wanted. Interestingly enough, my friend Brett Klein knew of an opportunity for me that ended up being my dream job—and through his connections, I got the job.

This is an important reason why keeping your connections alive is so important. So many people only reach out to others when they need something. I can smell that a mile away, and so can you.

As a result of nurturing that relationship, I created my own luck. I was prepared for the opportunity when it showed up, and I was in a perfect position to take advantage of it.

This is also why I work hard on my business whenever I make the time for it.

I create my Win It Minute videos every day because I value the consistency of my efforts. Doing the work every day leads to small wins, which can then lead to bigger wins. I spend hours preparing my topics for these videos, doing the research, and finally, filming them. These videos may change hundreds of people's lives, or perhaps just one.

But…what if the *one person* who sees a Win It Minute video is in a position to hire me to speak on stage. And what if that stage belonged to someone like Tony Robbins or someone else very well known?

People may hypothetically see me on his stage and think that I was "lucky". However, the truth would be that I did the endless hours of work behind the scenes preparing for that opportunity.

We see other people's highlights, but we don't see the hard work, or even the failures, that happened along the way.

It's not glamorous or sexy, so we never talk about it.

In order to get seen, I have to stay consistent in my efforts and put out hundreds of videos over a long period of time. That's when you have staying power.

Meeting my amazing wife worked in a similar fashion.

I was single and making an effort to build my network of friends, and one night some of those friends encouraged me to go out. After seeing this beautiful lady, I realized I didn't have the confidence to walk over and say hello right away. My friends gave me the confidence to take the chance and ask her to dance with me.

Was it luck?

I had to work hard to build that network of friends. Then, I had to work hard to go out that night because I wasn't inclined to do so. After that, I had to work hard to build the confidence to simply say hello and ask for a dance.

All of the time I spent networking and doing the inner work, I got a great result.

That one moment of insane courage led me to a new life, a new love, and beautiful marriage, and then having three kids who can ultimately change the world for generations to come—because we feed them hope, positivity, and confidence that *they are enough.*

Just like you are.

Was I simply in the right place at the right time?

Or did I work to put myself in the perfect position to take advantage of the opportunities that presented themselves?

Another great example is my son Adrian who had open heart surgery, as I mentioned previously. We worked hard because we didn't just settle for the first heart surgeon that we found.

This was an incredibly huge moment in our lives. And my wife was adamant about doing research and finding the very best heart surgeon we could find. Not all doctors are the same as you can imagine.

Our preparation met opportunity when her research led to a discovery that the University of Miami had just brought in the top pediatric heart surgeon in the world, Dr. Redmond Burke—and my brother-in law had just taken a new job there.

So, my wife convinced her brother to introduce himself to this heart surgeon, talk to him, and ask if he could volunteer to be on his team as an intern. The goal was to get to know him well enough that he could ask this world-class doctor if he would be willing to do heart surgery on his nephew if time opened up.

We ended up having the top heart surgeon in the world fall into our laps.

But it wasn't just luck.

It was because my wife convinced her brother to put in an extra effort to persuade the top heart surgeon in the world to take on his nephew's case. Some people think that we were lucky, but we weren't. My brother-in-law went to med school for 18 years and my wife convinced him to talk to the doctor.

All of these events came together at exactly the right time. The happy ending to this story is that the surgeon agreed to take our son's case and everything turned out great.

Because it was such a complicated procedure, we didn't just settle and just wait for luck to happen to us or for fate to intervene and take its course. We took control of the situation and put ourselves in the position to have luck come our way.

One final example that I want to illustrate happened during the real estate bubble in the late 2000's. At the peak of the housing market in 2006, we owned three houses—my wife bought two and I bought one.

Of course, we couldn't have predicted the collapse of the real estate market that happened a couple years later.

We were in our mid-twenties and were both making great money, but this put us in a financial crunch because now we were stuck with three houses.

While our friends were buying nice cars and jewelry, and taking exotic trips, we decided to focus on paying down the mortgages on our houses. It served as a forced savings account because we knew we had to pay a certain amount each month to maintain these three mortgages.

At the time, we viewed ourselves as completely unlucky because the market put us in a tough spot. But because we chose to be wise with our money during this time, we were in a better position to take advantage of the market when it rebounded.

When that finally happened, we sold one house, and that eventually led to the opportunity to build our dream house and move into it.

People may have called us unlucky. However, we kept working hard and put ourselves in a position to be *lucky* when the opportunity presented itself.

Not giving up is a huge component to this. When things look tough, it's important to assess what your options are, as well as the consequences of pursuing those options.

We made choices that turned out to be correct, and as a result, my wife and I were *lucky*.

CHAPTER SIXTEEN

HOW YOU CAN WIN YOUR DAY THE "WIN IT MINUTE" WAY

My hope not only for this book, but also for the Win It Minute motivational videos, is to help people realize the power that they have within themselves— not only to change, but how they can impact the world.

Our attitudes and behaviors are all about what we choose to input into our minds on a daily basis. As the great Zig Ziglar once said, "Your input determines your outlook. Your outlook determines your output, and your output determines your future."

It's important not to let other people affect our vision or perspective in life. We have a conscious choice to make our environment a product of who we are, rather than letting ourselves be affected by our environment as mentioned in a previous chapter.

That's a very important distinction.

I recently read an article that states how our attitudes and behaviors affect us and the people we interact with daily, whether it's our friends, family, or colleagues. Not only that, but our individual influence actually extends to others even if we are not in their direct presence. The fun part about this is that I have seen firsthand how true this is. When I do my Win

It Minute videos, I always hope that they impact someone. When people I don't even know message me to let me know that one of my videos made a positive difference that day, it encourages me to keep going.

A perfect illustration of this is expressed beautifully here:

Every action you take, and every word you speak to another person can have an amazing, ongoing ripple effect. In fact, your "Ripple Effect" will touch approximately 1,000 people today...so make it a beautiful one!" ---Mary Lynn Ziemer

It's amazing that our choices can impact that many people in a day. That makes our attitudes all the more important.

When you make the conscious decision to win your day, you're doing far more than improving your own well-being and opportunities to win every day. Your impact can profit the people around you, and consequently, their sphere of influence as they move throughout their days.

When I started this journey several years ago, this gave me a reason to learn and change my input. The biggest change I started to see was first in myself and then in others around me. It has given me a sense of purpose, and I think many people want to make an amazing impact on others around them.

But the biggest thing that you have to do is change yourself first. Michael Jackson famously sang about changing the man in the mirror first, and it's true. Initially, when I started creating a change within myself, and then within my circle of friends, the voices resisting these changes were strong from my friends and family at first. But that quieted down after the first few months of making the Win It Minute videos. Many people started to hear the message but the feedback slowed down.

Many people will quit in business or life when they don't see immediate progress or results. It's normal to want stuff quickly and immediately. But I chose to get started, and I kept doing the Win It Minute videos mainly because I was learning so much and I love that sense of purpose that it gave me.

Consistency is important when starting anything new. It took about a year of doing the Win It Minute videos before I got a lot of traction with them. Strangers started telling me that they had seen my videos and were positively impacted by them. Random people would approach me in social situations and tell me the same thing.

I started to experience the Ripple Effect in my own business, and was fun to watch happen. Those people providing me feedback gave me the fuel to get up early every day at 5:00am to read and learn. Sometimes I would have to spend six hours reading a full book to get one quote or get properly inspired for a one-minute video.

But if my efforts inspired one person, that made it all worthwhile. It fuels me to learn more and work harder.

This started out as a journey to teach and inspire. Interestingly enough, my kids have taught and inspired me more than anything. For example, when my oldest son was three years old, he became obsessed with Tarzan. We would watch the *Tarzan* movie together. If you haven't seen it, the story was all about the progression of Tarzan as a boy in a strange world. He was learning so many things, but he felt odd and excluded. He didn't feel like he was part of the community and he felt like he was different. Later on, he realized that his differences were what made him special.

Phil Collins has a song that I just love called *Son of Man* where the lyrics say, "In learning you will teach, and in teaching you will learn." Those words are profound because they made me realize what I was trying to do with the Win It Minute videos was teach others how to be inspired and have a positive attitude. But by doing that, I actually learned way more by trying to teach others and it was like a circle.

One of the best ways to change others is to try and learn first. And then you can teach people how to do things in a positive, uplifting way or even teach people how to do business or life.

I forced myself to learn and change myself in my quest to teach others. I started to create the brand that I wanted—the Win It Minute guy. And when I created that image that others saw me as in my videos, it made me also want to live up to that image and standardize that in real life.

For example, I'd be in a situation where I'd be upset or annoyed. I'm human like everyone else. Then I started asking myself, "What would the Win It Minute guy do in this situation?" And I would follow through on that.

This changed my life. I finally found a purpose concerning who I was and wanted to be, and it helped me work at it.

When you discover your passion, you should go all in. If your passion is baking muffins or even teaching the world how to bake muffins, go all in on that. If your passion is building cars, teach the world about how to fix cars.

Go all in!

It may take time to see the results, but the results come and you will learn along the way. That's the most important thing.

In life, you don't need to do videos to make an impact in the world. You can make an impact with your attitude and your mindset right where you are.

What started off as a journey turned into so much more for me and I've met so many great people. I'm inspired by more people than I can even count. I thought the Win It Minute would be about inspiring others, but inspired me more than anything.

I'm grateful for anyone that's ever watched a video, messaged me, or engaged with me about it as they are the fuel that keeps me going.

If you are one of those people, you've impacted my life more than you'll ever know.

The final chapter will contain thoughts and ideas that can help your journey become even more impactful.

CHAPTER
SEVENTEEN

WIN IT MINUTE POWER POINTS

Winning your day is so important, and it doesn't happen by itself. Taking steps to guard our hearts and our minds is critical to creating the results that you want in life. This final chapter highlights some of the things you can do to win your day and create what you want.

Build unshakeable confidence

Anytime we discover something we are good at, we often forget that there was a point in time when we had never tried it before. In fact, there's a very good chance we weren't good at that thing right away.

We build confidence with repetition. When I started doing my Win It Minute videos, I didn't know what to do. I simply had a passion to impact others around me. I built the mindset of doing something every day to move forward toward my goals.

I know that I have to start every single day with fueling my mindset to win each day. Pairing up a winning mindset with emotion is a powerful combination. If you walk into any situation with the right mindset, you can make anything happen. Others who don't understand your goals or your vision may put you down or ridicule what you are trying to do.

But you are a force of nature when you have the right goals, the right mindset, and the confidence to achieve anything you want. Those who put you down are unlikely to have the same goals and desires as you. When you have unshakeable confidence in achieving your goals, no one's opinion matters but yours.

They are interpreting your situation through *their* experience.

What they see as impossible is only impossible for *them*.

You can only control your thoughts and your perspective.

The most important thing you can do every day is to fill your mind with positive input. Make a list of your wins and review them frequently. This could mean writing down a list of 100 wins that you have experienced in your lifetime, or even writing down at least one win you had every day on a piece of paper and putting it into a jar. At the end of the year, you can review all 365 wins you had in the previous 12 months.

How can you not get fired up about that?

We tend to underestimate the good and overestimate the bad. Building confidence is about doing the opposite of that. Focus on the good. Doing so will guarantee that your light will shine bright.

Reminding yourself that you are a winner is the greatest way to keep being a winner.

Define your purpose

Most people go through life not knowing what their purpose is. They meander through life waiting for things to happen, rather than choosing to make things happen.

My purpose is to be the best version of myself so that I can inspire others. As I mentioned earlier, I really didn't have a distinct purpose in life for so many years. I was always known as an easygoing, nice, positive guy. Friends, family, and business associates would always comment about that.

But I didn't have that image of myself until I started the Win It Minute. At that point, I started to realize that there is a niche in the world for everyone. Once I found my purpose, I went all in on it. I found my purpose was to spread positivity and to be a light for others. I've learned that by being the light for others, you help yourself grow and shine even brighter by trying to light other people's candles.

And that's been the biggest aspect of my growth as a business person, as a friend, as a father, or with anything in life— realizing that I can control the environment with positivity and emotion. It affects almost every relationship I've had and every room I've ever walked into, and I've seen the effect of being the positive outgoing person regardless of what the other people are doing.

It truly affects each and every room I've ever walked into over the last few years. If I can leave a room better than I found it, that's a huge win. I can't control how other people respond to me, I can only control what I say or do.

My purpose is not dependent on what other people think of it.

And neither is yours.

Find whatever makes your heart sing each day. How can you make an enduring impact on someone else today?

What skills do you have that can create a lasting influence in the world around you? What do people typically compliment you on?

What gives you joy in life?

All of us have unique gifts and talents. Perhaps you aren't aware of them because you haven't looked for them.

Or maybe—just maybe—you haven't had people around you who are committed to seeing the best version of you. When you take your connections to the next level, it can make a dramatic difference in the trajectory of your life and career.

That's why having amazing relationships is so important.

Building and establishing amazing relationships

If you have ever read Dale Carnegie books, you know the best strategy to building relationships is to be interested in others more than being interesting. In other words, make everything all about the other person. It's human nature for each of us to care more about ourselves than someone else. The ones who truly stand out are the people who go out of their way to be curious enough to know more about someone else. Have you ever met someone for the first time and immediately upon being introduced you forget their name? It's because you were more concerned with your response to them and were not listening to their name. It's natural but once you recognize this you can make the change to listen better.

Anyone can talk about themselves all day long, but does anyone else *really* want to hear it?

How can you begin to do this?

Ask questions. Specifically, ask questions about the other person and their interests. One way to do this is to remember the acronym F.O.R.M., which stands for Family/Friends, Occupation, Recreation, and Motivation. These areas give ideas about what you can do to start a conversation. Most people love talking about their family, what they do for work, what they do for fun, and what their aspirations are.

It's a great way to find common ground with someone else, especially if you are meeting them for the first time.

The person asking questions is usually the person in control of the conversation, and when you get the reputation as a great listener, you will suddenly have people tell you what a great *communicator* you are!

I love talking to people about sports and business, so these are easy ways for me to connect with others.

Everybody has a passion point and it only takes about three questions, I believe, to find someone's. Some people make it their goal to tell you how great they are, so your goal should be to find areas of interest that they like discussing. Eventually, most people will realize how much time they spent talking about themselves and they will return the favor and start asking you questions.

It's also important to think well of others when conversations begin. If you believe someone is a great person, you will treat them that way, but if you have a pre-conceived notion that someone may not be the ideal person to interact with, self-fulfilling prophecy may kick in.

We tend to decide in the first couple of minutes how we feel about the person we are talking to, so be interested in the other person, don't simply try to be interesting.

This works when interviewing someone for a job as well. Both parties are trying to discover what the fit might be. It may not take very long to decide if the person might be a good fit for the company culture or not, and then you ask questions to validate or invalidate the initial assessment.

Have a championship mindset

The mindset is the most powerful thing that you can have to help you win your day. That was the first thing that I discovered on this journey, you have the power to determine your mindset.

And that all starts with the input you feed your mind and what you tell yourself. I saw a statistic that said someone is 86% more successful as a salesperson if they have a positive mindset. Even doctors, who are some of the smartest people we know, can be impacted by a positive mindset. There was a study that showed their diagnoses are 63% more accurate if they have a positive mental mindset.

Mindset determines everything.

And the beauty of it is we get to control our mindset every single day. Once you realize that you have the power of choice and free will, and ultimately it is your mindset, then you realize walking into any meeting or any relationship that you are the most powerful person there because you control your mindset.

Think And Grow Rich is a very impactful book that discusses mindset. Reading that book validated something that I always knew growing up but didn't *know*.

The power of the mastermind is a prominent topic in that book. If you are unfamiliar with the term, it means that a group of like-minded people come together to help each other achieve their purpose. When you have two or more people together, the effect is exponential. When you are in the *right* group, your business or career can take a quantum leap forward quickly.

People in a mastermind can be your peers or your mentors, and both are valuable for your journey. They can help you think much bigger than you ever thought possible. Once your mind expands its boundaries, it can never revert back to its original parameters.

But having a championship mindset only works when you take massive action.

So many people have great ideas. So many people have great intentions. So many people have to-do lists where if they accomplished everything they intended, they would be the most successful people that you ever met.

Most people don't follow through because they get caught up in everyday minutia and everyday issues, and putting out fires in their everyday life. But they don't get to their to-do lists.

We need to stop overthinking things and realize that action is the most powerful thing because too many people don't take action.

Even more importantly, taking action is something you must do repeatedly.

Athletes train over and over and over. It's not just about having the right mindset, but the habit of action that makes them winners. A professional basketball player may take 1,000 jump shots in practice. Repetition builds habits so that during the game at a critical moment, they don't even have to think about what they are doing—they have rehearsed that moment over and over again in their minds and in practice. Their body naturally knows the motion because the pattern of performance is clearly established.

Tom Brady is arguably one of the best quarterbacks in NFL history, not because he has the best reflexes or the strongest arm. He's the best quarterback because he's been in every situation and he's practiced it in his mind over and over. He's watched film for hours upon hours so that when he steps out on the field, he can just move into action without having to think about it as much because thinking will slow you down.

If you overthink something, you'll talk yourself out of it. And if you talk yourself out of action, you delay yourself, and you're 72% less likely to do it.

Find your crowd

It's been said that we are the average of the five people we are with the most, and it's true. The people you associate with have a dramatic impact on who you become and the direction your life takes. If you want to be fit and healthy, hang around with people who take their fitness and health seriously. If you want to be wealthy, hang around with people who have great wealth habits.

If you surround yourself with people who don't have clear goals, you will become that type of person.

Don't fool yourself. It's a lot easier for your average friends to drag you down than it is to lift all of them up.

One of my greatest strengths in life is that I have always been positive in my outlook on everything. I've always found great people to surround myself with, and I've had great friends who have always inspired me and led me in incredibly productive directions.

As I mentioned earlier, perhaps the darkest period of my life was when I first moved to Orlando and I was by myself. I didn't have a circle of influence or anyone to inspire me, motivate me, or teach me. I felt lost for about 18 months because I didn't have a network of friends.

This was pre-Facebook, so I didn't stay in touch very often with my close friends that I had left. I had gone from a close-knit community in Wisconsin where I was surrounded by friends and family every single day of my life, to being alone in a new city, not knowing anyone and not having that circle of strangers or friends. And it started my journey into the Win It Minute because it forced me to read and find inspirational books. That's when I discovered Zig Ziglar, Tony Robbins, and other motivational author and speakers. The messages they shared were the themes that were planted in me many years ago. That ultimately led to my learning journey.

Eventually, I found a group of friends and I worked hard to build those relationships because I knew the power of friendship and the power of surrounding myself with the right people.

And once you surround yourself with the right people, anything is possible. It builds your own confidence, and it helps build your competence. And as human beings, we're hardwired to be social, so the most important thing in the world is to get out there and meet people. There's a saying that 90% of life is just showing up. There are times we don't feel like stepping out of our comfort zone to find our crowd—we would rather stay home and relax. And for a brief moment, as author Seth Godin likes to say, your lizard brain tries to talk you out of it. But if you show up and connect with other human beings, there's nothing else that can replicate the high of connecting and socializing with others.

Find *your* crowd—the ones who share your goals, values, and attitudes. Find people who will help you get to the next level of whatever you want to achieve.

Life is too short to leave something like that to chance.

Have inspiring conversations with people every day.

That's how you win your day!

Overcome difficult times

It's no secret that all of us experience difficulties. Sometimes we start to believe that the tough times will never end.

In my experience, the most helpful thing that I focus on is having the mindset that it *will* pass eventually. Tough times don't last forever.

I would never make light of anyone's difficult situation, but the sun will rise the next day. If you are living and breathing, you still have a purpose to fulfill.

And if you can learn from it, those tough times weren't wasted.

In fact, if you keep encountering the same trial over and over, there's a chance that you haven't learned the lesson that is intended yet.

Think of video games where you win at level one and then advance to level two. That's a win, but level two is a lot more challenging for you. In fact, it's so challenging that you lose the game before you can move on to level three. You will never advance to level three unless you learn how to beat level two. That same challenge will keep reappearing for you until you *learn the lesson.*

Sometime we get so caught up in our own mess that we forget that others are in a worse place than we are.

I had the chance to experience that firsthand not long ago.

On that particular day, I was driving to a meeting and it was a two-hour commute. However, I encountered standstill traffic and it became clear that I was going to miss my meeting I was upset, stressed out, and angry facing the realization that I wouldn't make this meeting. I planned my entire day around and it was a four-hour round trip. That was the most important meeting of the day, and I had just lost a massive opportunity that this meeting would represent.

A few minutes later, I understood the reason for the traffic delay.

There was a huge accident on the side of the road, which resulted in a traffic delay of an hour and a half. So, my two-hour drive turned into three-and-a-half-hour drive and I didn't make my meeting.

And after seeing that accident, I was talking on the phone to my wife while waiting for traffic to pick up again. She asked, "How come you're not upset, how come you're not panicking?"

In that moment, as I saw the scene of the accident, I saw two mangled cars on the side of the road. I also noticed a child seat that was completely destroyed.

I thought to myself, "Holy cow, thank goodness that wasn't me—thank goodness that wasn't *my child!*"

As it turns out, I arrived to the meeting two hours late and the others had waited for me. I still had the chance to make the impact I desired.

Then I got to go home and see my kids that night who had no idea what just happened. And the next morning, I got to wake up and go to my kid's soccer game, fully appreciating what I had been given and what *didn't* happen to me.

There's no meeting or any amount of money that can replace your health and your life.

That's what my mind gravitates to when facing something tough.

As long as you have your health and the ones you love, you have everything.

Nothing replaces those things.

Never ever give up

If there's anything that I've learned from listening to audios or reading books, it's that persistence is critical. Nobody is an overnight success story, and no one is born successful out of the gate.

Everyone who achieves anything worthwhile has to work at their craft and work on themselves. Only the people who continue to work, move forward, and overcome adversity achieve success at the highest levels.

The idea of an overnight success story is a fallacy. Read a biography of almost any world-class achiever and you will quickly discover that they toiled for years trying and failing on multiple occasions. And the reason they are world-class achievers is because they didn't give up when most people would have.

But successful people keep going and don't let adversity take them down. We all face adversity every single day. But, two people may face the same situation and respond differently to it. I firmly believe 90% of life is how you react to it. And if you don't quit and you keep showing up and keep working at something, eventually good things happen.

But it takes hard work and persistence.

And I believe persistence starts with the mindset. The more you believe in your goals and keep working toward them, the greater the likelihood that you will eventually succeed.

I once read a statistic that salespeople who think they can make their quota are 97% more effective in their job. If you are in sales and you don't truly believe you can make your quota, you will be less likely to make the extra call because you don't think it will make a difference.

It works the same way with everything in life. If you have a positive mindset where you believe that something will work out for you, it will come to fruition and you'll succeed if you keep working at it.

Having faith in your outcomes is so important. It's the most powerful thing because it fuels to help you keep moving forward and never give up. The most powerful thing that you can do with your positive mindset is to maintain persistence and to keep moving forward so that you will see success.

Give back

"You can get everything in life you want if you will just help enough other people get what they want." -Zig Ziglar

Zig Ziglar is one of the writers and speakers who have influenced me the most. He wrote dozens of books about mindset, sales, leadership, and other personal development topics. The overarching philosophy that guided his teachings in contained in the quote above.

The key is helping other people get what they want first. So many people look out for their own interests first, and when you do the opposite of what everyone else is doing, you will immediately stand out from the crowd. And when you set yourself apart, people will gravitate to you and look to be in your world.

That's when you start to get the things that you want because reciprocity kicks in. When you do good to others, they will want to do good for you as well.

But here's the kicker—you can't do good to others with the *expectation* that they will reciprocate. That's not giving, that's a transaction.

However, when you give without expectation, great things start to happen and often in unexpected ways. Just because you give money doesn't necessarily mean you will get money in return. Instead, you could receive something you need much more at a critical moment.

The effect of giving, when done from a pure heart, can be intoxicating. There's no better feeling than to create an impact in the lives of people who need you in the moment.

Too many people lose sight of that, or perhaps haven't experienced it enough to realize that it's way more powerful to give and to help others than it is to receive. It's fuel for your mind and your body.

It's easy to lose sight of the innate goodness of people when all you pay attention to is the news or social media. But again, it's about purposely giving your positive input to see how amazing people can be.

One of the most selfless acts of love anyone can perform is to have a pet. You have to nurture and take care of it even though it can't reciprocate in the same manner that we give. We feed and take care of them, and what they give back is love and loyalty.

That's the best gift anyone can receive.

Your dog can't pay rent.

Your cat can't do your laundry.

Your hamster can't do your grocery shopping for you.

But when you give—not just to your pets, but to your family and friends as well—what you get back is far more valuable.

Volunteering is another way to give without expectation of receiving. Our society conditions us to be consumers, but when we give instead of take it can be life-changing.

If you ask anybody who has ever volunteered what their experiences have been, they will tell you that it's one of the best feelings in the world.

Perhaps people don't volunteer more than they do because they aren't aware of how powerful it can be. Feeding people, giving them a ride, or coaching a kid's sports team are all powerful examples of what volunteering can look like.

Everything that you have read in this book is designed to help you become the best version of yourself that you can be. A great way you can start your day is by watching my daily Win It Minute videos. You'll get a dose of energetic inspiration that will help you set the direction for your day unlike anything you have experienced before.

If you ever want to connect further, or watch the Win It Minute videos, you can visit www.thewinitminute.com. I would be glad to talk to you. Feel free to email at Keith@Winitminute.com as I would love to hear from and make a new friend!

Now, go Win The Day!

ABOUT THE AUTHOR

Being raised on the shores of Lake Michigan in a tiny Wisconsin town, Midwestern values were instilled in Keith Greiveldinger, along with the teachings of the great Vince Lombardi and his inspiration to Win The Day. Keith's career path started in a sales job with the National Basketball Association's Milwaukee Bucks and then took off from there. His passion for sales and sales management has led him to read countless books on motivation and psychology, and also to obtain an MBA from the University of Central Florida in Orlando, Florida.

Keith began his journey for the Win It Minute when his first child was born with a heart defect and needed open heart surgery. The emotional roller coaster inspired him to find the good in every obstacle, and he vowed to teach others the importance of desiring difficulties that allow you to have the mindset to Win The Day.

Keith is a highly engaging and award-winning sales evangelist with a record of surpassing sales objectives and leading others to high achievements. His keen emotional intelligence to bring a stylish approach to relationship building shows as he truly enjoys working with others. He is a connected leader with a strong emphasis on sales growth and a proven ability to boost any organization. He helps lead and build the winning mindset in many business leaders, sales leaders, and even athletic teams. Coach Keith, as he is passionately referred to in the community, has been passionately inspiring others to Win The Day for over 10 years in business, life, and sports.

His love for meeting people and believing in them is one of his greatest strengths, and he firmly believes in the power of creating relationships. After all, a wise man once told him that building relationships is the crux of life...don't ever forget that. By helping you Win Each Day, you can help others along the way Win Their Day. If you want to work with Keith, check out www.winitminute.com or email him at Keith@winitminute.com

Made in the USA
Coppell, TX
24 September 2021